"The principles of hypnosis when applied to copywriting add a new spin to selling. Joe Vitale has taken hypnotic words to set the perfect sales environment and then shows us how to use those words to motivate a prospect to take the action you want. This is truly a new and effective approach to copywriting, which I strongly recommend you learn. It's pure genius."

—Joseph Sugarman, author, *Triggers*

"Wow—*Hypnotic Writing* kept me awake last night! I planned to read for 15 minutes or so before going to sleep and ended up turning out the light when I noticed it was past 3 A.M. That's how powerful this book is. Sure, Joe gives you a world class education in the writing of copy itself, but that's just a start. What you really get is a deep understanding of how people think, feel, and act— yourself included. This knowledge is priceless in turning words into power, and ethically using that power to sell more of what you offer."

—Bob Serling, www.DirectMarketingInsider.com

"I've read countless books on persuasion, but none comes close to this one in showing you exactly how to put your readers into a buying trance that makes whatever you are offering them irresistible."

—David Garfinkel, author, *Advertising Headlines that Make You Rich*

"I am a huge fan of Joe Vitale and his books, and *Hypnotic Writing*, first published more than 20 years ago, is my absolute favorite. Updated with additional text and fresh examples, especially from e-mail writing, Joe's specialty *Hypnotic Writing* is the most important book on copywriting (yes, that's really what it is about) to be published in this century. Read it. It will make you a better copywriter, period."

—Bob Bly, copywriter

D0963913

"I couldn't put this book down. It's eye-opening and filled with genuinely new stuff about writing and persuading better. And it communicates it brilliantly and teaches it brilliantly—exemplifying the techniques by the writing of the book itself as you go along."

—David Deutsch, author, *Think Inside the Box*
(www.thinkinginside.com)

"*Hypnotic Writing* is packed with so much great information it's hard to know where to start. The insights, strategies and tactics in the book are easy to apply yet deliver one heck of a punch. And in case there's any question how to apply them, the before and after case studies drive the points home like nothing else can. *Hypnotic Writing* is not just about hypnotic writing. It IS hypnotic writing. On the count of three, you're going to love it. Just watch and see."

—Blair Warren, author, *The Forbidden Keys to
Persuasion*

"*Hypnotic Writing* has it all. It shows you how to master and accomplish the three things you need from your prospects. Attention! Captivation! Action! Never before has there been such a treasure trove of techniques for writing magnetic copy. *Hypnotic Writing* can be used immediately. It's an incredible desk reference tool. This is not a book you read and put up on the shelf for 20 years. It's on your desk where you can use it every day. I love *Hypnotic Writing* and I refer to it more often all the time. Joe Vitale is the world's first true and pure hypnotic marketer and this book will only bolster that fact. You will learn how to write headlines, openings, the power of perception change, and yes even secret laws of persuasion. I love this book. I encourage you to get your copy today and keep it away from your competitors."

—Kevin Hogan, Psy.D., author, *The Psychology of
Persuasion* and *The Science of Influence*

HYPNOTIC WRITING

HYPNOTIC WRITING

How to Seduce and Persuade Customers with Only Your Words

JOE VITALE

BICENTENNIAL
1807
WILEY
2007
BICENTENNIAL

John Wiley & Sons, Inc.

Published by John Wiley & Sons, Inc., Hoboken, New Jersey.
Published simultaneously in Canada.

For general information on our other products and services please contact our Customer Care Department within the U.S. at (800) 762-2974, outside the United States at (317) 572-3993 or fax (317) 572-4002.

Wiley also publishes its books in a variety of electronic formats. Some content that appears in print may not be available in electronic books. For more information about Wiley products, visit our web site at www.wiley.com.

Designations used by companies to distinguish their products are often claimed by trademarks. In all instances where the author or publisher is aware of a claim, the product names appear in Initial Capital letters. Readers, however, should contact the appropriate companies for more complete information regarding trademarks and registration.

Library of Congress Cataloging-in-Publication Data:

Vitale, Joe, 1953–
     Hypnotic writing : how to seduce and persuade customers with only your words /
Joe Vitale.
        p.   cm.
     ISBN-13: 978-0-470-00979-6 (pbk. : alk. paper)
     ISBN-10: 0-470-00979-9 (pbk. : alk. paper)
     1. Persuasion (Psychology)   2. Written communication.   3. Influence
(Psychology)   4. Business communication.   I. Title.
BF637.P4V58 2007
659.1—dc22

                                                                        2006020136

Printed in the United States of America.

10   9   8   7   6   5   4   3   2   1

To Robert Collier

AWARENESS MEANS I AM NOT
BODY NOR MIND

DESIRES & FEAR WHEN VANISH YOU
ALSO REALIZE THAT YOU ARE GOD

A TEST TO SEE IF BABA
USES HIS POWERS

TO HELP OTHERS OR

BENEFIT HIMSELF

AND THE ANSWER IS ONLY
TO HELP OTHERS AS
REVEREND ZIG ZIGLAR ALSO
SUGGESTS.

TO HELP YOU CREATE & DELIVER
VALUE
TO YOURSELF
TO YOUR SHAREHOLDERS
& TO EVERYBODY IN BETWEEN!

> All successful communication is hypnosis.
> —Milton H. Erickson, M.D.

> Words were originally magic and to this day words have retained much of their ancient magical power.
> —Sigmund Freud, 1915

> In what I call waking hypnosis, however, all four of these features are absent; sleep is not mentioned in the preliminary explanation to the subject; sleep is not suggested, directly or indirectly; the subject experiences neither drowsiness nor sleepiness, if we may trust his introspective account; and there are present none of the objective indications of drowsiness or sleep.
> —Wesley R. Wells, 1924

KRIYA ~~YOGA~~ 1/2 hour in THE AM +
1/2 hour in THE PM; 7 DAYS/WEEK
FOR 24 YEARS = ENLIGHTENMENT

CONTENTS

Author's Warning

The material you are about to read is based on a privately published book I sold to seminar attendees in 1985. I later updated and released the material in 1995, as my first e-book. It became an instant online bestseller. In 2004 I taught a private seminar based on the principles in this book. Attendees paid $5,000 each to sit at my feet and hear the secrets you are about to read. This book in your hands is an enlarged, revised, and updated edition of all my previous works on the subject.

Hypnotic Writing is powerful. Anyone who uses it will increase their ability to communicate and persuade, which can obviously lead to more sales.

But there are other reasons to use Hypnotic Writing than immediate sales. For example, a friend of mine is a medical doctor. He can't get everyone to follow his advice. Smokers keep smoking. Overeaters keep eating. If he knew some of the principles of persuasion that you'll learn in this book, he would be better able to up his success rate at getting people to do what is in their best interest to do. Whether he writes or speaks, he could use words in a more hypnotic way to get better results.

Also novelists, journalists, romance writers, e-mail writers, web site creators, and even blog writers can use Hypnotic Writing to capture more readers and keep them longer. The secrets in this book will help you make your writing stand out in the crowd. In this age of information overload, you need an edge. Hypnotic Writing is it.

This book itself is an example of Hypnotic Writing. Throughout this book you will find yourself going into a light hypnotic trance. Better stated, you will *not* notice you were in a trance until you *wake up* from it. In other words, you will become aware that you hadn't been aware. That's fine, as it means you were in a "waking trance" (which I explain later).

Obviously, this will not cause you any harm. I'm mentioning it so you become alert to the hidden mechanism of Hypnotic Writing at work, even in this very book, so you can begin to use it in your own writings later.

Please use this material for good. You cannot make anyone do anything against their will, so don't even try. Hypnotic Writing is for ethical businesspeople (or anyone else) who want to better state their case to their prospects.

Someone wrote me a nice letter, thanking me for my books but also taking the time to tell me she was "put off" by my use of hypnosis in marketing. She said it removed choice from people. She thought it was evil.

Since you may be thinking the same thing, let me point out a few facts:

* *Hypnosis never removes choice.* You can't be made to do something under hypnosis that you didn't already want to do while fully awake. For proof, just ask yourself if you buy everything I offer. Probably not. Yet I'm the father of Hypnotic Writing. Obviously, you used your power of choice to buy or not, despite any "hypnosis" in my marketing.
* *Hypnosis is not evil.* It is used by dentists, doctors, and psychologists to help people get more of what they want out of life. It's been sanctioned by the American Medical Association since the 1950s. Anyone still thinking hypnosis is evil is caught up in a cultural myth, which is a kind of trance all by itself.

So what is hypnosis?

My definition of hypnosis is anything that holds your attention. A good movie, or book, is a type of hypnosis. So is a good sales letter, or sales pitch, or infomercial. I'm not talking about manipulating minds; I'm talking about entertaining them. For example:

- *Britney Spears is pretty hypnotic.* But not everyone buys her music. (I don't.)
- *Dan Brown, author of **The Da Vinci Code**, is pretty hypnotic.* But not everyone buys his books. (I don't.)
- *Harry Potter has much of the world in a trance.* But not everyone buys the books. (I don't.)

Bottom line: Hypnosis is another tool. It does not control people and it does not give godlike powers to anyone. In marketing, it gives you an edge, but if you use it to try to sell a lousy product, it won't help you at all.

Kevin Hogan, hypnosis trainer and author of several books, including *The Psychology of Persuasion*, says, "Hypnosis makes life better in most every way. It gives a salesperson or marketer a decided advantage over the competition but not over the client."

You want to learn Hypnotic Writing because it helps you get and hold attention. It also makes you a much better communicator.

After all, if you aren't getting attention and you aren't holding it, you aren't doing *any* selling, are you?

—Joe Vitale, www.mrfire.com

ACKNOWLEDGMENTS

I want to thank everyone involved in creating this book, many of whom I'll forget to mention by name, so forgive me. Nerissa, my love, is my main support person and best friend. Matt Holt and my friends at Wiley are terrific people to know and work with. Blair Warren and David Deutsch are best friends and lovers of books. Suzanne Burns is my key assistant and publicist, and a positive influence in my life. Kevin Hogan helped me become a better hypnotist. David Garfinkel and everyone in my mastermind group supported me in this project, including Jillian Coleman-Wheeler, Cindy Cashman, Craig Perrine, Pat O'Bryan, Bill Hibbler, and Nerissa Oden. Mark Joyner was the first to believe in this book over 10 years ago, when it was a skinny e-book that made history online. Elsom Eldridge has shown his support of me and this material every year by asking me to speak about Hypnotic Writing at the annual National Guild of Hypnotists convention. Thank you, one and all.

INTRODUCTION

John Burton

Wow! Multilayered goodness in each piece. You think the outer layer is wonderful but then, as you delve deeper, you go to the center and find the most satisfying textures, savoring each uniquely flavored nugget. A new candy bar? No, no, no. Joe's new book, *Hypnotic Writing*, a "how to" manual, is just that and so much more. Joe not only describes *how* to do Hypnotic Writing with great details and guidance, he also explains what it is and why to use it along with countless examples of successful applications. You get to glimpse behind the scenes into the creation of Hypnotic Writing. And you get to learn how to do Hypnotic Writing for yourself as Joe guides and supports you through the whole learning process.

Just who am I to make such claims about Joe's book, *Hypnotic Writing*? I come from a field, not so far away, a field where I also explore, develop, and utilize hypnotic language. But I use hypnotic language differently from Joe. I hold a doctorate from Vanderbilt University in human development counseling and a master's in clinical psychology. I'm a licensed counselor and supervisor in Greenville, South Carolina, running my own private counseling practice. I've been a practicing counselor for over 20 years and a practicing human being for 51 years. I'm also certified as a clinical hypnotherapist. I co-wrote *Hypnotic Language: Its Structure and*

Use and was the sole author of *States of Equilibrium*. My next hypnotic language book is due for publishing this autumn. Now we find the convergence.

I hold a great fascination and appreciation for language and its amazing power. Words exist like winged energy, transporting us to places high and wide. Words link each of us together as human beings. Words can paint pictures, move us to tears or to joy. Words can expand our consciousness until there are no words for the experience. I have read and studied, practiced, and been in trainings with experts in hypnosis. Language is the vehicle that transports us to that wonderful otherworld, hypnotic trance. Here, we can do anything as everything is available.

Joe Vitale is an expert in his field. He has studied, read countless books and articles, and practiced and received trainings from linguistic and marketing experts. He uses this expertise to persuade consumers to purchase particular products or services. Some might say that the category of marketing or sales and the category of psychotherapy exist in a mutually exclusive way. But I can safely say that while sales is not therapy, therapy *is* sales. So I am familiar with this interesting process and its dynamics.

Perception, motivation, and values combine to create choice. Language in general and hypnotic language in particular, written or spoken, can provide the necessary perceptual shifts, access motivation, and lead toward satisfying choices. Choice may exist as the way our free will manifests. Joe skillfully and effectively identifies and works with these principles and dynamics that exist within each of us. And he does it with love, yes love! Joe does not stoop to low-level and transparent tricks in his work. He rises to higher levels of being in order to bring love into the equation. I believe this element of love provides the difference in what works over the long haul with consistency. After all, love is what we each seek. Love rules. As William Law stated, "Love is infallible, it has no errors, for all errors are the want of love."

Joe accomplishes many feats in this book. He does not make you meet him where he is; he meets you where you are. This makes it so much easier for the reader, you. Joe does what good teachers do. He helps you identify your current style, ways of thinking, and beliefs. He provides exercises to encourage getting in touch with your thoughts, perceptions, and goals. And imagine this: He induces a trance in the process! Throughout this whole work, Joe masterfully invokes trance after trance so that you will gain insight and more deeply understand Hypnotic Writing. Experience is not just the best teacher. It may be the only teacher. Reading this book gives you the experience of Hypnotic Writing. This all leads to your *mastery* of Hypnotic Writing. But this process of gaining mastery includes more than just writing hypnotically.

Another significant quality of this book is that you don't just learn Joe's Hypnotic Writing. You learn how to do this for yourself, how to make Hypnotic Writing your own. Joe does not suggest you mimic him. He does not want you to write from rote! He shows you how to launch off in your own direction, drawing on *your* inner creativity. How does Joe do it? Well, this brings us to another powerful dynamic recurring throughout this book.

The book presents the material in such a way as to makes the unconscious conscious. Hmmm, now that's an interesting notion. Just what the heck is that, the unconscious becoming conscious? Some of you may have experienced your conscious mind becoming unconscious. But with Joe's book, he writes in a way that increases your awareness, not just by providing you with more information. Joe lifts the cover off the unconscious processes used in Hypnotic Writing. Now you can see, understand, and utilize these potent principles in your own writing.

The genius of the master hypnotherapist, Milton Erickson, was apparently so natural to him that Erickson himself could not or would not fully explain the processes he used in hypnotherapy. Many experts studied Erickson's hypnotherapeutic ways so that others could understand the processes and utilize them as therapists. In this book, Joe identifies and illuminates the many attributes of effective Hypnotic Writing. You don't have to wonder what qualities are present in Hypnotic Writing. He lists them clearly. Joe provides examples and practice exercises for you to gain familiarity with them.

Yet another accomplishment happens in this book. Joe not only shows you how to write hypnotically, not only shows you how he does it, not only helps you develop your own style, but (whew!) he provides you with references to numerous experts who know Hypnotic Writing and the mental-behavioral principles driving it from within. He shows you, trains you, and then points you toward resources that you can use to further enlighten and train yourself. The result is that you gain the knowledge and master the know-how to become an accomplished hypnotic writer. Oh, and one more thing. You must practice. Only practice as much as you want to get good at Hypnotic Writing.

John J. Burton, Ed.D.
Author, *Hypnotic Language*
and *States of Equilibrium*
www.DrJohnBurton.com

1

IT'S TIME TO AWAKEN

"You are getting sleepier ... sleepier.... As I count backward from 10 to 1, you will feel your eyelids getting heavier ... and heavier. ..."

That's the image you probably get when you think of hypnosis. And you're right. Hypnosis is about getting you so relaxed that your mind, especially your subconscious, is more receptive to commands. Hypnosis is controversial but effective. It's been around since 4 B.C., and for good reason. It works. To understand Hypnotic Writing better, let's begin with a little history.

IN THE BEGINNING WAS THE TRANCE

According to William Edmonston in *The Induction of Hypnosis*, trance states and the seeds for hypnosis began with the ancient Hindus. Later, ancient Greeks in the fifth century B.C. used "sleep temples" to help cure people. Most of the other ancients, including the Romans, used words to create spells. They also usually placed their hands on or over people to move the "magnetic energy" within them.

In 1765 Franz Anton Mesmer, generally (and inaccurately) considered the father of "mesmerism," opened salons where patients applied magnets to afflicted parts of their bodies. Later Mesmer moved to Paris where he further developed his theory. He became very popular. He wasn't using hypnotism per se, but he was using words to create suggestion, probably unknowingly, to influence his patients.

In 1784 Louis XVI set up a commission to investigate Mesmer. It included Benjamin Franklin, M. La Guillotin, and Antoine-Laurent Lavoisier. They concluded that magnetism *with imagination* had some effect, but Mesmer's magnetism and magnet healing theories were discredited.

Le Marquis de Puysegur believed magnetic power was produced in his own mind and was transferred to the patient via his fingertips. He found that he could produce a sleep in which the patient would follow his commands.

In 1841 the British doctor James Braid saw a demonstration of mesmerism by a Frenchman named La Fontaine. He was impressed, and started using the mesmerism techniques in his practice. He used a shiny bright lancet case to induce his patients to enter a deep "hypnotic sleep." In that state his patients would accept his suggestions. He coined the word *Neurypnology* (literally 'nervous sleep'), from Hypnos, the Greek god of sleep. This was the first use of the word *hypnosis*.

Dr. Braid didn't care for magnetism, believing rather in "fascination" (fixation) and verbal suggestion. He also instituted the use of hypnosis as anesthesia for both minor and major operations.

In 1884 Dr. Ambroise-August Liebeault of France proclaimed that he could cure people in a hypnotic state by suggestion. In 1886 he was joined by Professor Bernheim from Paris, and together they published *De La Suggestion*, which further rejected the concept of magnetism.

During World War I, between 1914 and 1918, the Germans realized that hypnosis could help treat victims of shell-shock. It allowed soldiers to return to the trenches almost immediately. A formularized version of hypnosis, called Autogenic Training, was devised by Dr. Wilhem Schultz.

After World War II, Milton Erickson—arguably the most famous hypnotist of all time—had a major impact on the practice and understanding of hypnosis and the mind. He theorized that hypnosis is a state of mind that all of us are normally entering spontaneously and frequently. As you'll soon see, this has enormous implications for your ability to influence people through your written words.

On the heels of Erickson's work, hypnosis evolved into a well-respected practice, used by doctors, psychologists, business and law enforcement personnel, and even by people in sales and marketing. It's also used for self help and self improvement. With the development of self-hypnosis, one doesn't even need to rely on a therapist any longer.

Hypnosis is a tool, not a cure in and of itself. It is used for stress management, stress related disorders, dental and medical anxiety, and anesthesia, even in obstetrics. It is also used for pain management, as an adjunct to psychotherapy, and in the management of a wide range of phobic, anxiety, and other medical and psychological problems.

It's being used by dentists, doctors, and therapists as well as stage hypnotists. It's been sanctioned by the American Medical Association since the 1950s. It's been used to help people with a variety of problems, from psychological to physical ones.

HYPNOTIC WRITING

But none of the above is Hypnotic Writing.

You don't want your readers to fall asleep and neither do I. By "Hypnotic Writing" I mean writing that is irresistible. Writing that rivets your eyes to the page. Writing that is so clear and concise and effective that you can't resist reading all of it. And more than that, Hypnotic Writing gets you to remember—and act—on what you've read. Hypnotic Writing is spellbinding, unforgettable, and filled with embedded commands.

That's a lot better than putting your reader to sleep, isn't it?

I believe you've come across Hypnotic Writing at one time or another. Think back to the last time you were totally focused on a letter or a book. Did you lose track of time? Did someone call you, but you didn't hear them yell out? Were you so absorbed in your reading that nothing else mattered?

Face it. You were hypnotized.

Even Shakespeare used Hypnotic Writing, though of course he would never have called it that. According to Peter Brown, in his book, *The Hypnotic Brain*, Shakespeare's *The Tempest* uses hypnotic induction to get readers captivated. The play begins with a shipwreck, causing people to sit up and take notice. That's a key element in hypnosis: Get attention. Shakespeare did it. The play then moves into a dialogue where the audience is told to sit still and listen. That's a hypnotic command. Brown adds, "The story is as absorbing and moving today as it was nearly four hundred years ago."

One of the readers of my books wrote me one day to tell me a book he had read hypnotized him to stop smoking. He said Allen Carr's book, *The Easy Way to Stop Smoking*, actually awakens people from their trance of addiction. By the time they finish reading the book, they are nonsmokers. Apparently Carr's Hypnotic Writing works, as he has now helped millions of people stop smoking. Many people said just *reading* the book will help you stop smoking.

Friends told me the same thing happened when they read *Healing Back Pain* by John Sarno. Again, apparently just reading the book helped them awaken from the "pain trance" and actually alleviated and in many cases cured their back pain. I had a similar experience while reading Sarno's latest book, *The Divided Mind*. It seemed to take me from one trance—believing in the power of traditional medicine—and to put me in another trance—believing in the power of the unconscious mind. This is the power of Hypnotic Writing. (I explore this trance state in my next book, *Buying Trances*.)

In fact, in a few pages I prove how one of the greatest mystery writers of all time actually used hypnotic techniques in her books to make her readers buy more of them. In short, she made readers addicted to her novels.

I love Hypnotic Writing. I long to read books that capture my attention and won't let go. Actually, I don't see enough writing of that caliber. Do you?

If you want to hold your reader's attention, then you have to learn how to create Hypnotic Writing. That's what this book is all about. My intention is to reveal—for the first time anywhere—the principles and strategies that will transform your writings. In an age when radio, television, computer games, videos, and movies are screeching for our attention—and when there is more information than you can possibly read—you must learn to write material your readers can't avoid. You don't have any other choice.

With these Hypnotic Writing concepts in mind, you'll begin to write memos, letters, ads, reports, and yes—even books—that few can resist. You will be able to create mesmerizing writing. You will become a superwriter! You will be equipped to develop writing that outshines the competition and dazzles your readers!

And with your new ability, you'll be able to get more results and command higher pay for your work. "Hypnotic Writing," in short, will give you the edge you need to create successful and powerful writing.

Hypnotic Writing isn't about manipulation; it's about communication. You won't put your prospects or buyers into trance states where they do your bidding. People will never do what they don't have a latent desire to already do. The idea behind Hypnotic Writing is to help you better communicate, and thus better persuade people.

All of this will become clear as you move through this book.

Are you ready?

You cannot teach a man anything; you can only help him find it within himself.

—Galileo

2

STOP!
DO THIS FIRST

How do you currently write your sales letters, e-mails, ads, or web site copy?

You already have a strategy for writing. For this book to make the most sense to you, you need to know where you're at right now. In short, become aware of your current writing method. From there, it will be easier to adapt what you are about to learn.

On the lines following, write a brief explanation of how you currently go about your writing. Explain *your* process. What do you do just before you write? What do you do *as* you write? What do you do after you write? Write your answers here:

_____

_____

_____

_____

_____

_____

_____

_____

_____

_____

_____

_____

3

WHAT IS IMPOSSIBLE?

A few minutes ago I read about a woman who has 6 children, 35 grandchildren, 75 great-grandchildren and 10 great, great-grandchildren—who jumped from an airplane to celebrate her ninety-third birthday. That's a woman who thinks big.

I believe in the impossible. I think you can have, do, or be anything you can imagine. That's the subject of one of my earlier books, titled *The Attractor Factor*. It's also, for the most part, the way I live my life.

I love to think big. I also love to read about people who set "impossible" goals, and then achieve them. Whether it's Roger Bannister breaking the four-minute mile, NASA sending a man to the moon, Bruce Barton writing a fundraising letter that pulls a 100% response, or a 93-year-old woman skydiving, all of it proves we have no known limits. None.

What we have, instead, are mind-sets, or mental models. Yoram Wind and Colin Crook, writing in their mind expanding book, *The Power of Impossible Thinking*, declare, "Mental models shape every aspect of our lives."

For example, I am currently reading C.K. Prahalad's book, *The Fortune at the Bottom of the Pyramid*, and love the true stories of people and companies helping the poor in places like Brazil and India. These people are not thinking small.

For example, Aravind Eye Hospital in India grew from an 11-bed facility to the largest eye care facility in the world. They see over 1.4 million patients and perform over 200,000 sight-restoring surgeries each year. Two-thirds of their patients are served at no cost, and those who pay, pay an average of just $75. The hospital was modeled on the management style of McDonald's—only it gives fast care for low (or no) money.

Here's another example:

Casas Bahia grew from one man selling blankets and bed linens door-to-door to the largest retail chain in Brazil. They sell electronics, appliances, and furniture. With its emphasis on serving the poor customer, its low prices and credit determined by payment history rather than formal income—70% of Casas Bahia customers have no formal or consistent income—Casas Bahia grosses over US $1 billion and has invoked total loyalty in its customers.

I feel most of us don't think big enough. Not even close. To help s-t-r-e-t-c-h your mind, read Prahalad's book just mentioned and read *The Power of Impossible Thinking* by Wind and Crook.

Wind and Crook explain that our mental models of the world are what stop us or help us. Thinking there is no profit in helping the poor is a limited mental model. The people in Prahalad's book have moved beyond limited thinking.

With all of this in mind, what do you want to accomplish from studying *this* material? What's your "impossible" dream? What would you want, if you knew you could not fail? Whatever it is, write it down here:

_____

_____

_____

_____

_____

_____

4

A Disclaimer

I've been writing for almost 40 years. I've been teaching writing for over 30 years. I've read hundreds of books on writing, written a dozen or so myself, and have taught and spoken about writing for decades.

Still, I don't know it all. Neither can I put everything you need to know into one book, even if it is a book I've worked on night and day for months, that's based on my entire life's education and experience to date.

That said, please know that I strongly advise you to read other books on writing. A few treasured classics are listed in the back of this book. Many of my articles can be found on my main web site at www.mrfire.com. A search for books on writing at www.Amazon.com will keep you busy for years with the pages and pages of titles it will return to you.

If all you want to know is Hypnotic Writing, then by all means read this book, the books listed in the Bibliography, and invest in two other key sources:

1. My Hypnotic Writing Wizard software. See http://www .HypnoticWritingWizard.com.
2. My entire library of hypnotic e-books. See http://www .HypnoticLibrary.com/g.o/10386.

I've made this book as easy to follow as is humanly possible. I've distilled the Hypnotic Writing method into something you can understand and implement.

The rest is up to you.

Ready to get started?

5

A Beginning

> My aim is to put down on paper what I see and what I feel in the best and simplest way.
>
> —Ernest Hemingway (1899–1961)

PULL UP A CHAIR AND

I'm considered the creator of Hypnotic Writing. While it's true that I wrote the first book on the subject (okay and the next seven e-books on the subject), I have to confess that I learned how to write "hypnotically" from two unusual sources.

I used to read Jack London, Mark Twain, Shirley Jackson, and Ernest Hemingway and marvel at their ability to weave words in such a way that they moved me to laughter, fear, or tears.

How did they do that? We have access to the same alphabet and same vocabulary as those masters, yet they wrote classics and most of the rest of us write garbage.

What's up here?

Then, I would read sales letters by Robert Collier, or Bruce Barton, or John Caples and wonder how they used the same language but caused people to shell out their hard-earned money—often during tough economic times.

How did those famous copywriters do that? How did they write to persuade?

My obsessive curiosity led me to investigate both kinds of writing. I studied literature throughout college and for years afterward. I minored in English and American literature. I loved Nathaniel Hawthorne, Herman Melville, Jack London, Mark Twain, William Saroyan, and others.

I wrote fiction, plays and poetry, trying to adapt what I was learning and did pretty well at it. I was published a fair amount. And I saw a play I wrote, *The Robert Bivens Interview*, produced in Houston in 1979. It won an award, too, in the first Houston Playwrights Festival.

Years later, I studied copywriting. I read everything I could get my hands on, from in-print marketing books to out-of-print collectibles. *The Robert Collier Letter Book* changed my life. The works of John Caples opened my eyes.

I spent time practicing what I was learning, writing sales letters that sometimes bombed, but more often broke all records—some of them on the verge of being miraculous. My letter for Thoughtline, an old DOS program, is still being talked about today. (You'll find it later in this book.)

The result of this foot in two worlds experience led me to create what I later coined "Hypnotic Writing."

That didn't happen overnight, of course. It took well over 20 years of cooking within me before the recipe was ready. And it wasn't until I had read the book *Unlimited Selling Power* before everything came together for me.

That's when I wrote a book that became the beginning of a movement. I used to sell that book in the back of the room at my talks in Houston, way back in the 1990s. That book later became my first e-book. It's now sold in the tens of thousands online. The title is *Hypnotic Writing*.

Generally speaking, Hypnotic Writing is any writing that holds your attention. Hypnotists call it a "waking trance" (which I explain in a minute). John Burton, in his advanced book *Hypnotic Language* writes: "All communication invites the receiver into a hypnotic trance."

Note he said *invites* a person into a trance. You can start writing something and bore people, which is a trance you don't want to invite people to experience.

You can start talking to someone and that will invite them into a trance, too, but if you are boring, their mind will not stay with you.

My definition of Hypnotic Writing is:

"Hypnotic Writing is intentionally using words to guide people into a focused mental state where they are inclined to buy your product or service."

The kind of writing I do in my business of copywriter and marketing consultant usually means I'm writing to sell. That means Hypnotic Writing is any writing that holds your attention long enough to get your money.

I don't mean that to sound blunt. I'm a results oriented kind of guy. I think you want to know how to write to sell, too, else you wouldn't be reading this book.

So let's be honest with each other. You want to know how to write the kind of words that make people buy your product or service. You aren't trying to start a cult or sell snake oil. You believe in your product or service. You want to help people and you want to make money as you do.

Right?

Me, too!

6

AGATHA CHRISTIE PROVES HYPNOTIC WRITING EXISTS

D id mystery novelist Agatha Christie literally hypnotize her readers?

Consider: According to a British television documentary aired in December 2005, scientists from three leading universities studied 80 of the famed novelist's works and discovered she used words that invoked chemical responses in the brains of her readers.

The study—called The Agatha Project—involved loading Christie's novels into a computer and analyzing her words, phrases, and sentences. The scientists concluded that her phrases trigger a pleasure response. This causes people to seek out her books again and again, almost like an addiction.

According to the study, Christie used literary techniques mirroring those employed by hypnotherapists and psychologists, which have a hypnotic effect on readers. This is clear evidence that the principles you're going to learn in this book truly work.

The study found that common phrases used by Christie act as a trigger to raise levels of serotonin and endorphins, the chemical messengers in the brain that induce pleasure.

I've been saying this for years. Certain words and phrases push buttons unconsciously in people. They respond without being aware of it. I've been teaching people how to improve their sales letters and web site copy with these very insights for over 30 years. Apparently Agatha Christie used Hypnotic Writing to make her books—as one scientist unhypnotically said—"unputdownable."

It sure worked for her. Agatha Mary Clarissa Christie (1890–1976) is possibly the world's best-known mystery writer. The Guinness Book of Records lists her as the best-selling fiction author of all time with over two billion copies in print in the English language. Obviously, Hypnotic Writing helped her.

The study went on to report the following about Agatha's writings:

Favorite words or phrases, repeatedly used in a "mesmerizing" way, help stimulate the pleasure-inducing side of the brain. They include *she, yes, girl, kind, smiled,* and *suddenly.*

George Gafner declares that certain words lead people into trance states in his book *Hypnotic Techniques for Standard Psychotherapy and Formal Hypnosis*. He says such words include *wonder, imagine,* and *story.*

Again, to me, this isn't news. There are similar words and phrases in marketing that set off brain activity—and later buying activity.

Do you know what they are?

Probably not.

Few people do.

But they are revealed in this book.

Imagine: You are about to learn the proven ways to use words to put people into what I call a *buying trance*. This is a hypnotic state of focused attention where people are riveted to your message and more inclined to do what you ask—such as buy from you. I tell you in this book story after story of how others use this skill. As you read, a sense of wonder will awaken within you.

Did you note the hypnotic words smoothly used in the paragraph you just read?

Take another look:

Imagine: You are about to learn the proven ways to use words to put people into what I call a *buying trance*. This is a hypnotic state of focused attention where people are riveted to your message and more inclined to do what you ask—such as buy from you. I tell you *story* after *story* in this book of how others use this skill. As you read, a sense of *wonder* will awaken within you.

Hypnotic Writing is almost invisible. You don't see it in action unless you've been trained to look for it. For most readers, all they experience is a need to read. With this book, you'll help awaken in people a need to buy.

Agatha Christie secretly encouraged people to buy her books with Hypnotic Writing. You're about to learn how to make people buy your product or service—with words alone.

Imagine the possibilities!

7

MY SECRET TO HYPNOTIC WRITING

I magine someone hands you the following message:

"*Riguardo a gli dice il mio segreto di dollaro di milione per scrivere di copia di vendite. Questo è qualcosa non ho mai detto nessuno altro nel mondo intero. Lo dirò giustamente adesso, se lei promette a tiene quest'un segreto. Stato d'accordo?*"

You wouldn't be too interested in it, would you? It would look strange. Confusing. You might assume it's from another language, but unless you knew Italian, you would only be guessing the language and the message.

What would you do? Obviously, you would need to translate the message.

How? In this case, you might just go online at a great web site for translating languages, enter the above text, and quickly discover that those words in Italian actually mean:

"*I'm about to tell you my million-dollar secret for writing sales copy. This is something I've never told anyone else in the entire world. I'll tell you right now, if you promise to keep this a secret. Agreed?*"

Ah! Now it all makes sense! Now you know what the words mean and you are free to enjoy them, act on them, or just dismiss them. But at least now you've gotten the communication. Relax. Breathe. Smile. Ahhhhhh . . .

But what does all this translation business have to do with how I write hypnotic sales letters, ads, and news releases?

In a nutshell, translating is *exactly* what I do in writing sales copy. When someone hands me a technical manual on a new software program—with the idea they want me to write a sales letter for the software—what I do is translate that manual.

In short, I do the same thing the language translation web site does. I simply look at what the manual says the software does, and then I translate it into benefits that make sense to you, the consumer. In a way, the manual is written for techies, much like Italian is written for Italians. I have to translate both so you can understand and make sense of them. If I don't, you won't care.

Here's an example of what I mean:

Recently I was hired to rewrite a brochure. My client handed me their draft. It read well. There were lines such as, "When was the last time you felt okay?" Well, nothing wrong with that. It works. But I found a way to translate it into something more meaningful, understandable, and emotional. And I did it with just one word. I wrote, "When was the last time you felt fantastic?"

The translated line communicated better. It's the difference between hearing the line in Italian or in English. As Mark Twain put it, it's the difference between lightning and the lightning bug.

But maybe that example is too simple.

At another point in their brochure they were trying to explain the concept of suppressing emotions and how suppression could be harmful. Their words were fine, just as Italian words are fine. But they didn't communicate in a way most people would hear. So I translated their words to,

"Suppression is building bombs. When you bury an emotion, you bury it alive."

See the difference? I do this with all my copywriting. I take what I'm handed and translate it into benefits, clear language, and bottom line emotion. This truly does feel like translating languages to me. And like learning any new language, it takes time to master.

I take the copy given to me, turn on the part of my mind that knows how to speak copywriting, and I translate the words in front of me into words *you* can understand.

I also do this copywriting translation with news releases. For example, last month I was hired to write a news release for a woman's book. I could have written a headline that said, "New Book Explains How to Communicate Better," which is what the book is about. But that's Italian. It doesn't speak in emotional terms or in a way most editors want to hear.

After doing some research and learning more about the author, I translated the headline to instead read, "Female Pentagon Advisor Reveals Tips to Success." The latter is far more intriguing. All I did was translate her book into news. I took it from Italian to English. I took it from English to Emotion. I took it from words to power.

What's the secret to being a good "copy translator"?

I could probably quote a relevant line from any number of books on marketing. But I'll grab one from a 1965 book I just received today. It's by Robert Conklin. The title is *The Power of a Magnetic Personality*. He wrote: "Putting it simply, it means this: Every time you state a fact, describe how that fact will benefit the other person."

There you have it. It's what I've been saying for years: "Get out of your ego and into your reader's ego." Translate what you want to say into simple words and concepts that make sense to your readers.

I hope I've done that with this brief chapter. I began with the idea to tell you how I write sales copy. But I didn't want to just say, "I translate all words into sales copy," which may or may not make sense to you. Instead, I wanted to describe, with examples, what I do so you truly comprehend it. Finally!

"Adesso che lei sa il mio segreto, va avanti e traduce le sue lettere di vendite, l'advertisements, e le liberazioni di notizie nell'ones che farà lei milioni dei dollari. Piacere!"

Translation: "Now that you know my secret, go forth and translate your sales letters, advertisements, and news releases into ones that will make you millions of dollars. Enjoy!"

8

You Can't Even Bribe Me to Read a Lousy Letter!

In 1994 I taught a workshop to 10 people on Hypnotic Selling and Hypnotic Writing. (See www.HypnoticMarketingStrategy .com.) Each paid $5,000 to be there. I began the event with the following story:

> I got a FedEx package yesterday and I want to read the letter that came with it. First of all, it came by FedEx, so that was pretty attention getting in itself. It had a $20 bill attached to it. Pretty attention getting, too. I'm going to take a look at this. It begins:

> Dear Joe Vitale:

> I have an offer that I would like to share with only you, that will make you a stack of those $20 bills in one to two weeks. Before I go on, let me explain why I am sending this to you.

Then he goes on to say, "My name is," and I won't say his name.

Then he says, "I am in a jam and need to make $10,000 before the end of the month. There are three reasons why I need this: one, to keep a promise to a close friend. I told a close friend that I would have a motorcycle before he gets back from his deployment in the desert."

He goes on to explain that, "Two: I made some bad decisions with money a while back and I'm currently very tight with money. In other words, broke," is what he says.

"Three: I'm on vacation from the 13th of this month until the 29th and I would like to be able to do something over that time period. I would at least like to be able to visit my grandparents in Fort Worth and have enough money to enjoy it."

He tells me where he lives. He then goes on to say he wants to create a joint venture with me.

On the second page he describes himself as being a marketing specialist and that he wants me to send out a mailing to my list, looking for people who want his services. He says, "I will charge a retainer fee up front, anywhere from $5,000 to $25,000, depending on how much of a profit I think I could make for their business.

"That is with anywhere from 5 to 50% of the profits generated. The retainer will be paid off on the back-end profits." Then he goes on to say, "I will give you 50% of all the profits." He gets down here and asks me to call him and so forth, and gives me his name and number. One of his P.S.s says this:

"If you are wondering why there is a $20 bill attached to this letter, it is because I hope to be sending you a large stack of them in the next several weeks."

I then looked at the 10 people in the room and asked: "Is this a hypnotic letter?"

I got a yes, I got a no, I got a maybe.

What do you think?

Was the letter hypnotic?

To me, this is not a hypnotic letter.

In fact, it is a terrible letter. I sent his $20 back, because he said he's broke. The only reason I did not burn this is because I need his address, which is on the back of the second letter, so I can send it back.

Why isn't it a hypnotic letter?

My observation is, first of all, he got my attention, which is one of the key ingredients for writing good copy. He FedExd it to me; very important. Twenty dollars: very eye-catching.

It begins well: "I have an offer that I would like to share with you that will make you a stack of those $20 bills in one to two weeks." That's good; he's speaking to me.

However, from there it is all about him. The first statement was something to the effect that he wants to buy a motorcycle. I do not care if he needs a motorcycle. He wants to buy it because he made a promise to a friend. I do not care that he made a promise to a friend.

The second one is that he has made bad decisions about money. He is broke. I do not care about that. I would care, probably, if he told me in different terms, but a lot of people are broke. He's telling me that he is broke and he wants to do something that is off-the-wall.

Third is that he is on vacation. I do not care if he is on vacation. He wants to make use of his vacation time and make some money. Then he is asking me to do a mailing to his list, and he is claiming he is a marketing specialist. Where is the proof that he is a marketing specialist? So, this is full of doubts.

I am just thinking that this guy doesn't know what he's talking about. Then he wants to charge people on my list $5,000 to $25,000 to do marketing, which is what I do! Why would I send my people to him and then let him get half of the money that all should go to me?

None of this makes sense. Of course, there is his P.S.: "If you're wondering why there is a $20 bill attached," he wants to help me make more. That is pretty good. However, it's powerless at that point, because he lost me with all of this self-serving stuff.

Obviously, a letter written with Hypnotic Writing would be focused on me, not him. By the same token, this is a clue for you to remember: Hypnotic Writing occurs when you get out of your ego and into the reader's ego.

9

WHAT IS HYPNOTIC WRITING?

Recently I spoke at the world's largest hypnosis convention. Two thousand professional hypnotists from all over the world came to hear me describe Hypnotic Writing. I told the crowd that Hypnotic Writing is a form of *waking hypnosis.*

"Waking hypnosis" is a term coined by Wesley Wells in 1924 and first published in the book *An Outline of Abnormal Psychology* in 1929. He wanted to separate the idea of hypnosis as conscious sleep with hypnosis as awake concentration. In other words, traditional hypnosis thinks of someone with their eyes closed but aware; Wells proposed that someone could have their eyes *open* and still be subject to hypnotic suggestion.

Later in his 1964 book *Hypnotherapy,* Dave Elman defined waking hypnosis as: "When hypnotic effects are achieved without the trance state, such hypnotic effects are called waking hypnosis."

Waking hypnosis is not magical or mystical. It's no different from being absorbed in a good movie. Or being riveted by a good book. Or driving down the highway for hours and being "zoned out." In each instance you are in a waking trance.

A waking trance is a concentration of attention. You are focused on something before you, to the exclusion of virtually all else. Whenever you read a fascinating book, you are engaged in a mild trance. Because your eyes are open, this state is called a *waking trance.*

In 1956 an anonymous hypnotist, writing in his famous mail-order course, *Dynamic Speed Hypnosis,* declared: "Anything you do which makes your listeners react because of *MENTAL IMAGES* you plant in their minds is *WAKING HYPNOSIS!*"

Just replace "listeners" with "readers" and "waking hypnosis" with "Hypnotic Writing" in the sentence you just read and you have a good working definition of Hypnotic Writing. It would read like this:

"Anything you do which makes your readers react because of *MENTAL IMAGES* you plant in their minds is *HYPNOTIC WRITING!*"

Of course, the kind of Hypnotic Writing you and I want to do is focused on making a sale. That's why my definition is: *"Hypnotic Writing is intentionally using words to guide people into a focused mental state where they are inclined to buy your product or service."*

Again, Hypnotic Writing is a form of *waking hypnosis.* It is characterized by a focus of attention. It is a trance state where you are wide away but focused on something you are reading.

Hypnotic Writing achieves this state by the right use of words to create mental experiences. In other words, you get people so interested in your web site, or e-mail, or sales letter, that almost nothing else matters. And if you do this right, your Hypnotic Writing will lead your readers to take action.

All of this will make sense as I walk you through some of the secret steps and insights of how to create Hypnotic Writing.

But first, let's look at an example of Hypnotic Writing.

Take This Test

See Figure 9.1 for a picture of a massage pen.

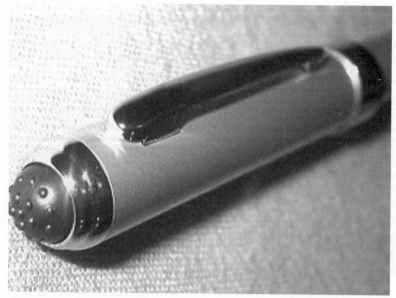

Figure 9.1   A Massage Pen

Basically, it's a regular pen—it writes—and the tip of it (shown), also has a massaging head on it. Press it against your skin and you get a massage. I know it isn't much to go on, but how would you write a paragraph to sell this pen?

Write it here.

_____

_____

_____

_____

_____

_____

_____

Now, here is how one web site describes the massage pen:

Product Description

The unique metal ball-point pen with built-in massage.

Rugged metal construction.

Attractive design.

Patented massage function.

Replaceable ink refills.

Batteries included.

Well, is that Hypnotic Writing?

I don't think so.

It has the facts, but it doesn't have any reason, or benefit, for you to care about the facts. Result: boredom.

Now, here is how the lively copywriters over at http://www .Stupid.com describe the exact same massage pen:

IMAGINE you had a teensy-weensy masseuse to carry around in your shirt pocket. Any time you desired, you could order your minimasseuse to soothe your tired muscles and rub away your tensions. Now imagine this tiny masseuse had a pen sticking out of his head and ran on batteries.

Well, you're not likely to come across a miniature, penheaded masseuse—but here's the next best thing. Introducing the world's first MASSAGING PEN!

Is that Hypnotic Writing?

You bet!

Before you go on, note your observations about the "stupid" description.

Why do you think it was hypnotic?

_____

_____

_____

_____

_____

_____

10

HYPNOTIC WRITING: A CASE STUDY

My friend Pete Siegel showed me this copy, which he wanted to use on a web site. Look at it and tell me what you think.

> **Discover Why The Country's Foremost Success Hypnotherapist *Continues* to Help So Many Enjoy "Unexplainable" Breakthroughs, and Truly *Massive* Personal Gains!**
>
> **For 26 Years, His Claim of "I'll Help You Move from Ordinary to *Extraordinary*!" Has Been Proven to Help Millions Worldwide Enjoy Amazing Life Transformations; He *Guarantees* You'll Make Staggering Confidence, Incredible Personal Income, and Peak Life Performance Your Everyday Fact!**
>
> **You're About to See That His Acclaimed, *Mega*-Personal Development System Will Work as Thoroughly and Decisively—for *You*.**
>
> **Yes—Now You Can Go On to Produce the Simple, Yet Stunning Personal Change That *Makes* Life Say an Overwhelming *Yes*—to *YOU!***

(Read On!)

Hey—are you getting all you can—all you want to, all you believe you **should**—out of yourself every day, doing targeted things to prosper and purposefully move yourself **ahead**? If not, **why** not!

Is your confidence, motivation, focus, and sense of capacity for serious improvement—for **success**—where it should be, indeed, where you know you truly **need** it to be, for you to start making **megagains** in your life? If not, **why** not!

Are you naturally mentally programmed to exert the quality, irresistible effort that steadily, decisively moves you into greater personal increase, personal triumph—and personal income? If not, **why** not!

Even though you say you work "hard," try "hard," and/or strive to improve consistently—do you find it seems you're sort of just "going through the motions"—seemingly stuck at levels of "same old, same old"? Or "Okay"? Or even "good"? But **not** seeing or feeling you're making the kind of progress you want to, sense you should, indeed, deeply **know** you should? If so, **why**!

Are you finding that decisively reaching your personal development and financial goals seems to be **elusive**. That pride laden, joy overflowing, richly substantive **success** filled life you see others possess still seems to be a far-off case of "Want it, but for some reason **aren't** getting it" for you? If so, **why**!

And are **you** becoming more—notably, **decidedly** more? Is your life steadily becoming richer and more rewarding **because** of your daily efforts? Indeed, are you growing, increasing, advancing, and succeeding in **multiple** areas of your life **because** of the kind of hopes, dreams, and continual life effort you expend? If not, **why** not!

Now, stop for a moment, and think here—and **really** get a sense of just how commanding you and your entire life **would** be if you had all the preceding aspects set and working the way you really **wanted** them. Well, you can do more than just think about this now, because:

You'll Now Go Ahead and Fully Take *Charge* of the Mental Factors to Bottom Line *Success* In These Areas. Is This Do-Able? Yes. Is It Do-Able by You—*Absolutely!*

See If You Want the Following to Start Characterizing *Your* Life

- Incredible self-confidence?
- Empowering self-esteem?
- Boldness and directness projected outward from feelings of solid self-worth?
- The ability to decide upon an ***increased*** income or financial goal—and to then strategize, work toward, and achieve it (***fully***)?
- Efficient action and peak life performance that produce overwhelming ***success*** results and outcomes?
- Full, free, wholly genuine communication impact?
- The affinity to easily, comfortably connect with ***quality*** people—and form lasting, positive relationships?
- The ability to ask for something—and ***get*** it?
- Feeling in ***control*** of your destiny, instead of being at the mercy of other people's thoughts and whims?
- Reflecting the talent and discipline that efficiently follow all the way through with a task, project, or requirement—until it's conclusively, ***successfully*** completed?
- Awakening each day calm, positive, and filled with an uplifted spirit—and ***success*** expectations about your upcoming day?
- Taking that ability, potential, and capacity for excellence you ***know*** you have, and actualizing (bringing it forth) into tangible, empowering, real-life fact?
- Feeling mentally strong, emotionally strong, and filled with the dynamic energy moving you to recognize, seize, and then to ***convert*** opportunity into decisive personal gain?
- Feeling a genuine, surging motivation and confidence to start speaking up, acting up, and start doing for your***self*** what you know you've been leaving up to others?

- Finding your *true* place in this world—your *purpose*—and richly living it, and enjoying all the relationships, money, joy, and fulfillment it has connected to it?
- Being forever free of your negative past (and its life compromising tendencies)?
- Releasing, *forever*, tendencies toward blocking, limiting, and/or sabotaging yourself—and enjoying new, self-tailored affinities that build you *up*, empower you, and efficiently move you *ahead* in your life?
- Reflecting the mind-set that regularly takes the initiative to ensure that your vital health, personal advancement, and perfect self-expression continues *demonstrably*?
- Looking within yourself and finding answers you've heretofore been haplessly looking for (and *not* finding) outside yourself!

Success—*Your* Success—Is Never an Accident
but the Result of Regularly Applied Strategies,
Actions, And an Internal Framework
That Fully Overcomes the "Small You"—
and Engages Life Vitally as the *Maximum* You!

Now here's how I rewrote his copy, making it more hypnotic:

Discover Why the Country's Foremost Success
Hypnotherapist *Continues* to Create
"Unexplainable" Breakthroughs,
and Truly *Massive* Personal Gains
in people just like YOU!

For 26 Years, His Claim of
"I'll Help You Move from Ordinary to *Extraordinary!*"
Has Been Proven to Help Millions Worldwide
Enjoy Amazing Life Transformations;
He *Guarantees* You'll Make Staggering Confidence,

**Incredible Personal Income,
and Peak Life Performance Your Everyday Fact!**

**At Last: Gain Iron-Will
Self-Confidence—Destroy Your Inner Limits—
Develop a Power Mind and quit pussyfooting
around with your life and get RESULTS!**
*Guaranteed by the world's
foremost sports hypnotherapist!*

Now, at last—Get his three ***PowerMind*** worldwide best sellers combined into one brilliant ***Mega***-life transforming system— Read on for details.

Would You Like Any of the Following?

- Incredible self-confidence?
- Empowering self-esteem?
- Boldness and directness projected outward from feelings of solid self-worth?
- The ability to decide upon an ***increased*** income or financial goal—and then strategize, work toward, and achieve it (***fully***)?
- Efficient action and peak life performance that produce overwhelming ***success*** results and outcomes?
- Full, free, wholly genuine communication impact?
- The affinity to easily, comfortably connect with ***quality*** people—and form lasting, positive relationships?
- The ability to ask for something—and ***get*** it?
- Feeling in ***control*** of your destiny, instead of being at the mercy of other people's thoughts and whims?
- Reflecting the talent and discipline that efficiently follow all the way through with a task, project, or requirement—until it's conclusively, ***successfully*** completed?
- Awakening each day calm, positive, and filled with an uplifted spirit—and ***success*** expectations about your upcoming day?

- Taking that ability, potential, and capacity for excellence you **know** you have, and actualizing (bringing it forth) into tangible, empowering, real-life fact?
- Feeling mentally strong, emotionally strong, and filled with the dynamic energy moving you to recognize, seize, and then to **convert** opportunity into decisive personal gain?
- Feeling a genuine, surging motivation and confidence to start speaking up, acting up, and doing for your**self** what you know you've been leaving up to others?
- Finding your **true** place in this world—your **purpose**—and richly living it, and enjoying all the relationships, money, joy, and fulfillment it has connected to it?
- Being forever free of your negative past (and its life compromising tendencies)?
- Releasing, **forever**, tendencies toward blocking, limiting, and/or sabotaging yourself—and enjoying new, self-tailored affinities that build you **up**, empower you, and efficiently move you **ahead** in your life?
- Reflecting the mind-set that regularly takes the initiative to ensure your vital health, personal advancement, and perfect self-expression continues **demonstrably**?
- Looking within yourself, and finding answers you've, heretofore, been haplessly looking for (and **not** finding) outside yourself!

**Success—*Your* Success—Is Never an Accident but
the Result of Regularly Applied Strategies,
Actions, and an Internal Framework
That Fully Overcomes the "Small You"—
And Engages Life Vitally as the *Maximum* You!**

Write down as many things you notice that make this new copy different and better.

_____

_____

_____

_____

_____

_____

_____

_____

11

THE GREAT INTIMACY SECRET

You should notice something about the "stupid" web copy you just read, as well as the before and after copy you read.

You should note the same insight about these very words you are reading right now. In fact, you should notice this characteristic in virtually all Hypnotic Writing.

What am I talking about?

Intimacy.

As you read those earlier words from the stupid.com site, you probably sensed a personality behind the words. As you read these words here, by me, you probably get a feel for my personality.

This secret is one of the greatest keys to creating Hypnotic Writing. People buy from people they like. When you allow your personality to come through, people feel a sense of intimacy with you. They begin to trust you. And like you. Rapport is built. And sales happen.

All of the great copywriters that I can think of wrote in their own voice. They didn't try to be someone else. David Ogilvy wrote like David Ogilvy. Dan Kennedy writes like Dan Kennedy. Joe Vitale writes like Joe Vitale. I don't try to be Dan or David, and they don't try to be me.

This lesson is of enormous importance. What it means is this:

Forget trying to imitate any writer you admire. (*Note:* Studying other writers is a wise way to learn how they wrote. I just don't want you to *become* another writer.) Forget trying to please English teachers. Erase everything you ever learned about "how to write."

From now on, you have my permission to write in any way that feels right to you.

If your style is to use slang, then use slang.

If you are from a different country, let that uniqueness come forth.

If you like to tell funny stories, then tell them.

Your style is your voice, and your voice will create an intimacy with your reader that is profound.

Now note: I am not advocating being mindless in your communication. I will teach you my persuasion formula in this book. By writing in your own style, by following my formula, you will create Hypnotic Writing. It will just be *your* Hypnotic Writing. Not mine. Not anyone else's. Yours.

I can't stress this enough. What people want is a new voice. They want to read words from a trusted new friend. That can be you.

Here's a million dollar secret: Many great copywriters call a friend and tell them about the product or service they want to sell. They record the call. They then play it back, listening for the ways they described what they were selling.

Why did they do this?

When people think of writing, the inner pressure gets turned on. All their past education comes rushing in, almost drowning their creative voice.

But when they speak, they are loose. Mark Twain said, "If we were all taught to speak the same way we were taught to write, we'd all stutter."

Hypnotic Writing comes from being loose. It comes from not editing yourself as you write. It comes from trusting yourself, being yourself, and expressing yourself.

It comes from being *you*.

12

WHAT'S MORE
IMPORTANT
THAN COPY?

I don't want you to get hung up on writing. It's important but it's not *that* important. Let me explain it this way:

There are three keys to the success of any direct marketing campaign, whether it's done online or off:

1. *The list (or the traffic).*
2. *The offer (or the deal).*
3. *The copy (or the Hypnotic Writing).*

Out of the three, copy is the least important.

For example, just this past week I completed an e-book on RSS and Blogging, new technologies online. I mentioned the e-book in my recent newsletter. Even though the web site for the e-book isn't done, and the sales letter isn't up, so many people rushed to the site, ready to buy the e-book, that my sweet co-author gently said, "Ah, Joe, maybe we should rush things along."

I thought about it and said, "Just throw something up online, saying we don't have a sales letter yet, but if you can't wait and want the book right now, click here."

She did. You can take a look at it in Figure 12.1.

Figure 12.1   The Stampede Secret Web Site

I then sent out this quickly written e-mail:

Subject: This *has* GOT to be the wildest thing I've ever seen.

All I did was *mention* how to create a stampede of traffic with a new RSS tool, and people drove to the site at http://www.stampedesecret.com to order.

The thing is—we weren't live yet. We didn't have a sales letter up or even the ordering system turned on.

I told Laura—my co-author—to just slap something up on the site, turn the ordering switch on, and to open for business today.

I'm going to go out of business as a copywriter when people want something so bad they don't even need the sales letter for it, but if you can't wait either, go see— http://www.stampedesecret.com.

This one will go down in the history books.

Go for it.

Dr. Joe Vitale.
President, Hypnotic Marketing, Inc.
Author of way too many books to list here.
See www.MrFire.com or www.Amazon.com.
Member BBB Online 2004.

As you can see, there isn't much copy, but what's there is designed to create excitement and curiosity, two key ingredients to Hypnotic Writing.

The result of our "no sales letter" marketing campaign?

I tested this letter to one of my smaller lists. We made one sale almost instantly. (Laura was so excited she nearly called me to scream, "*WE MADE A SALE!*")

Of course, I'll eventually put a full-scale sales letter on the site. When I do, I'll mention that people were so eager for this new e-book that they didn't even need a sales letter to encourage them to buy it.

But the truth is, a sales letter is essential. Why? Here's a quick answer: When people went to the site and then clicked "order," they were suddenly faced with the price of the e-book: $97. Most people aborted right then and there.

A good sales letter will *prepare* the reader for the price, and then give it in a soft, convincing way. That's why you need a sales letter. It does the persuading. A "no sales letter" site means *no sales.*

My point here is this: Copy is important, but it's not *the* most important element of your results matrix. You need a terrific offer, and a list or traffic that wants that offer. Writing copy after that should be a snap.

Remember: ***List/Traffic*** + ***Offer*** + ***Copy*** = ***Success***!

(Check http://www.StampedeSecret.com to see what sales letter we finally used.)

Now don't think you can make sales without Hypnotic Writing either. The following case study will prove what I mean.

13

HYPNOTIC WRITING CONTROLLED STUDY

Just in case you're still skeptical and need proof that Hypnotic Writing exists, consider the following. Brad Yates is a master at EFT, or Emotional Freedom Techniques. EFT is a method for tapping away psychological issues so you are free to have, do, or be what you want.

Some people call it "psychological acupuncture." You use a finger or two to "tap" on certain areas of your body, which releases stuck energy so you can move forward without any internal blocks.

Snicker if you like. EFT has been used for well over 10 years and is now practiced by tens of thousands of people. They can't all be faking problems and then faking resolutions. EFT works.

Brad Yates was one of my guests when I did my Attract a New Car teleseminar a while back. I liked him and told him about an idea I had for a series on Money Beyond Belief. It would be a course to help people remove their barriers to having money. Brad would teach people EFT so they could remove their blocks to receiving money.

Brad loved the idea, we conducted the seminars, and then quickly put up a web site to sell the audios. Now, Brad knows EFT but he doesn't know marketing, so the site wasn't the strongest in the copy area. The words left something to be desired. I offered some advice but didn't have the time to rewrite the site. So we left it alone and opened it for business. You can see it at http://www.bradyates.net/page45.html or just below and at the pages that follow.

MONEY BEYOND BELIEF!

Moments from now, you could be transforming your relationship to money, creating greater freedom to attract as much of it as you desire!

Are you ready . . .?

If you're struggling with money, it's not your fault.

Parents, society, movies, and even your friends are programming you to stay in a poverty mind set.

They aren't doing it on purpose. They aren't evil. They were simply programmed and are passing the virus down the line, to you.

You are not stuck—there is something you can do about it.

The latest tool from Joe Vitale and Brad Yates to help you achieve the breakthrough you want is a pair of transformational teleseminars on Money Beyond Belief.

These calls were designed to help you remove the hidden beliefs stopping you from receiving the money you seek.

If you're ready to have Money Beyond Belief, then *order right now*.

What you will receive are recordings of two calls in which limiting beliefs about money will be neutralized—over two hours of powerful life-changing material.

In these calls, you won't simply be given more information. To a great extent, what keeps you from enjoying more prosperity is not a matter of what you don't know—it isn't a matter of needing to read a few more books, attend a few more wealth-building seminars, and so on.

What stops you is the information you already have that isn't working for you. The limiting beliefs about money—"rules" you have developed about what you need to do—or whom you need to be—in order to have wealth. Rules about why you can't have it.

Note: They aren't *the* rules—they are *your* rules. Unnecessary rules that have nothing to do with being a good person. Rules that many very good people—happily for them—do not have.

If it means allowing more wealth into your life (which, as you will see, actually benefits others as well), isn't it time to break some of your rules?

You will hear amazing information that may very well be new to you, but these calls are also experiential. In the next 2+ hours, you will be led through hands-on exercises that will leave you positively changed at a deep level.

The calls were super! I love those guided imageries at the end. Brad takes an exciting set of techniques and splashes in a giant dash of intuition and creativity. Result—he probes problems and leads you easily through issues you never even knew were preying on you."
—Charles Burke, www.Synchronicity-Secrets.com

I'm totally psyched about this process! I feel very differently after the calls, and I fully expect two things:

1. I will keep using this process.
2. This clearing will turn into *lots* of money and great outcomes for me very soon!

—Amy Biddle, http://spiritual-healing-secrets.com

This is the response of one of the participants on the call—and this is after just one listening! Once you have downloaded the MP3s, you will be able to listen repeatedly—and you will want to!

With each listening, more clearing takes place, and the empowering feelings—and the powerful effect they have on your ability to create, attract, and allow wealth—are enhanced!

Read the responses, and know that anytime you want to replicate those feelings—and even exceed them—you can do so!

The programming you received from others created beliefs about money—most likely beliefs about why you couldn't or shouldn't have it—and certainly not an abundance of it.

> The calls were wonderful! They were sooo powerful!! Thank you for your willingness to conduct them. These techniques are a moment-by-moment tool when needed. I am so very pleased that I have been trained how to do it. When any sort of negative thought comes—well, it is neutralized within seconds. As I am a fan of Joe's, I am becoming a fan of Brad's. Thank you for following your callings. It is a benefit to all of us. Awesome!"
>
> —Joyce McKee, www.joycemckee.com

Whether you realize it or not—and whether you are willing to admit it or not—these beliefs are blocking your ability to experience and enjoy greater abundance.

How much money could you enjoy once you get beyond your current limiting beliefs?

Well, the calls were amazing and very impressive! It was absolutely the *best* description and explanation about how this works! During Brad's intuitive guidance, I "watched" as beliefs that I had acquired in childhood got chipped away. And then (as if watching from the outside) saw the *core* of the restrictive thinking revealed and quickly start to dissolve—the "Achilles heel" was uncovered. There's more for me to do, and with the help of pros like Brad and Joe, I see that the Universe's abundance is here for me, too! Brad and Joe, thank you for your generosity of time and spirit!"

—Carol S.

In the first call, we clear up false beliefs about money itself, such as:

- Money is the root of all evil.
- People with a lot of money are bad.

If you are harboring any negative beliefs about money, is it any wonder more of it doesn't show up?

In the second call, we tackle false beliefs about you in relationship to money, such as:

- I don't deserve money.
- I'm not good (smart, talented) enough to have much of it.

If you're ready to be free from those limiting beliefs, then *order right now.*

Of course, these limiting beliefs are repeatedly replaced during the exercises with empowering beliefs, such as:

- I am more than good enough to have an abundance of money.

- I am worthy and deserving of an abundance of all good things, including money.
- I can do a lot of good with money.

The exercises in these calls are designed to leave you knowing and feeling that these statements are true (and—they are!).

If you're ready to feel *really* good about yourself and your relationship to money, then *order right now*.

The potential value of these calls is—well—beyond belief. Obviously, we could easily charge $100 or more.

But we want to make it easy for you to have Money Beyond Belief—we want everyone to have this—basically, we want to change the world. So the price, for the time being, is set at *only $49!*

If you're ready for it to be easy to have Money Beyond Belief, then *order right now*.

Want more?

Well, we want more for you!

If you order today, you will also receive the following bonuses:

Because you are going to enjoy this work so much, we are also throwing in two additional teleseminars: Tapping into Abundance and Tapping into Vibrant Health. That's two additional hours of clearing the blocks to an abundance of health, wealth, and happiness! Previously only for paid subscribers on the calls (for $30), this is the first time recordings are being made available—and they are yours free with the purchase of Money Beyond Belief! ***Order now.***

Take a moment and look at the site.

* What do you think of it?
* Is the copy strong?
* Is it hypnotic?
* What's missing?

And here's the million dollar question:

Does the copy make you want to buy the product?

Brad and I told our lists about our product. We stood back and waited for orders.

And waited.

And waited.

Orders trickled in.

Weeks later, we still didn't have enough orders to make either of us very happy. We ended up using EFT on our disappointment.

While I wanted to rewrite the site, I just couldn't get to it with my books, projects, media appearances, travels, and more. Thank goodness a young copywriter by the name of Sam Rosen came to Brad and offered to help. Sam had studied all of my Hypnotic Writing materials and was game to prove his skills.

Sam completely rewrote our site. You can see the new copy at http://www.MoneyBeyondBelief.com or just look at what follows.

If you want to create *money beyond belief* the spiritual way—even if nothing's worked for you in the past:

Give Us 151 Minutes, and We'll Show
You 9 Ancient "Taps" that Lead to
Breathtaking Wealth and Abundance
—or You Don't Pay a Penny.

Each Tap Lasts Just 3 Seconds. We'll Walk
You Through Over 217 Combinations—
But Just One of Them Can Transform
Your Relationship to Money Forever.

Hard to believe? Let us prove it to you. If our *Money Beyond Belief! Home Tapping System* doesn't heal your deepest beliefs about money, we'll refund 100% your purchase (yes, that's cash back in your pocket— how's that for abundance?) on the spot.

Just imagine what it will be like to *wake up every morning and know you hold the "master key" to abundance*. Your body will glow with warm light because you've finally found the right mind-set to achieve limitless wealth.

And the best part is, once you complete our program, you'll *attract financial abundance* in ways that are completely in alignment with your highest spiritual principles. Finally, you will be firmly *in control* of your *spiritual and financial destiny*.

And even after you finish the program, all it takes is a minimum of *5 minutes and 49 seconds per day* to continue multiplying your "wealth mind-set," over and over again.

Take a moment and look it over.

Now here are the same questions as before:

- What do you think of it?
- Is the copy strong?
- Is it hypnotic?
- What's missing?

And here's the million dollar question: Does the copy make you want to buy the product?

Here are the results:

The first web site, which we call exhibit A, bombed. It barely made 100 sales in 100 days.

The second web site, exhibit B, blew down all the doors and made $8,500 in sales in only one day.

So does Hypnotic Writing make a difference in selling?

Consider:

- The product was the same.
- The price was the same.
- The audience we promoted it to was the same.

The only change was the writing.

Please note: The *only* change was the copy.

The next time you scratch your head and wonder if Hypnotic Writing will help your sales, re-read this chapter.

And then expect money beyond belief.

14

How I Learned the Secret of Hypnotic Writing

Few people know this, but I learned a lot about writing hypnotic copy from reading magic catalogs.

I've been interested in magic since I was sixteen years old. Inspired by Houdini, I wanted to be Harry Excello, the world's greatest escape artist. I used to let my brothers tie me up in the basement in Ohio. I always broke free. I knew Houdini's secrets. I could do what he did. One day I even considered being tied up and thrown off a bridge in my home town, left to struggle under water while I worked myself free from my binding.

That's when I turned to card magic.

I invented a few tricks and saw them published in magic magazines while I was still a teenager. But my father never approved of magic, and I let my interest hide under a mental rock for almost 30 years. Today I'm back into it. I've met Lance Burton, Peter Reveen, and Mark Levy, and famous entertainers like Kreskin use my marketing ideas. I'm now a life member of the Society of American Magicians, the group Houdini started in 1902.

I love reading magic catalogs because they are usually wonderful examples of hypnotic copy. In short, they sell the sizzle, not the steak. They focus on the benefit, not the feature. They always hide the secret. They always sell the dream.

These are important lessons.

One description might say, "Watch your audience explode in laughter when you produce a duck from your bare hands. No experience necessary. Easy to do."

That's hypnotic. It focuses on what you the magician want—to be the popular entertainer with no hard work to accomplish it.

Let me give you a longer example and dissect it for you.

Welcome to the Denny & Lee Magic e-Newsletter

Scott Alexander "Final Answer" Bill in Lemon

I have been waiting for this to be finished for quite some time now. Scott Alexander, the manager of our Denny & Lee Magic Studio in Las Vegas, has created quite a name for himself with the release of his two DVDs, *Midnight Show* and *10 O'Clock Show*. That was your first introduction to Scott Alexander.

The preceding sets the credibility level high. He's done DVDs before. He's the manager of a magic studio. This is no armchair magician. This is a pro. This copy creates trust, a very powerful ingredient in Hypnotic Writing.

Now he has released his version of the Bill in Lemon. These will be ready to ship in about two weeks. Due to the limited number of pieces in the first run, we are taking preorders for these units as they are sure to sell out very quickly. That's where being a subscriber to our newsletter pays off. These units will *not* be sold in every basement dealer's "Internet office."

This paragraph milks the famous scarcity principle to the hilt. When something you want is hard to get, then you *really* start to want it. When Gene Schwartz's famous book on advertising, *Breakthrough Advertising*, showed up on eBay, it sold for $900. Why? Because it was rare and dearly sought. Years ago I wanted a hard-to-get book on the bullet catch, a dangerous act in magic. The harder the book was to find, the more I wanted it. I almost became obsessed. When I finally had found the book, I was disappointed. It wasn't so hot after all. The preceding copy is letting you know this item is going to be rare and hard to get. That's hypnotic, as it pulls your psychological strings.

> This is a highly professional piece of apparatus exactly as used in Scott's professional program. Invented by a pro, performed by a pro, sold by a pro. Everything made in the U.S.A. under high-quality specifications. No imported junk!!

Sad to say, many of the gimmicks in magic are junk. They're poorly made. They break. Denny & Lee know this, so they are letting you know this piece of magic apparatus is going to be first-class.

> Without question, Scott Alexander has created the finest solution for the classic Signed Bill in Lemon ever devised. It's got it all. It's very easy to do, totally practical, fools everybody, and the audience goes wild!

You should catch on to what this copy is doing here. It is painting a mental picture of you performing this effect and being the life of the party. "The audience goes wild" is a phrase all magicians want to experience. It appeals to your ego. Talk about hypnotic. Appeal to your reader's ego and they will do virtually anything you ask. Think of the power this gives you!

> It's the classic effect—a borrowed, signed bank note is vanished or destroyed and appears inside a lemon. "The Final Answer" is designed for professional use. It meets and exceeds all of the test conditions.
> Yes—the signed bill really does end up inside a real lemon!
> Yes—the lemon can be in the audience before the bill is borrowed and signed!
> Yes—the audience can choose any lemon from a bowl of lemons!

Yes–the lemon can be sealed inside a zip-lock bag and never touched by the performer!

Yes—the spectator can actually cut the lemon open!

Two things going on there: First, they are answering all your questions. As you'll learn later in this book, anticipating objections and concerns and answering them at the right moment are keys to Hypnotic Writing.

Second, they are getting you into a yes mind-set. Look at all the yes statements. As you'll soon see, you can't create a hypnotic state without agreement.

First, let's talk about the gaff. It's been honed to perfection through countless hours of fine-tuning by Scott, Thomas Wayne, and Bob Kohler. Although it appears to be a common object, nothing could be further from the truth. In reality it's a precision made piece of machinery designed for stealth. Manufactured to our exacting specifications by master craftsman Thomas Wayne, you will marvel over the precision and gasp at the application. Objects this clever are usually reserved for James Bond!

A "gaff" is a device, gimmick, or trick. The copy here is letting you know, again, that this is high-tech stuff. And the association to James Bond is clever. Most people think of 007 as the collector of cool gadgets. It's very hypnotic to lead a person's mind to the right association you want them to make.

This diabolical gaff will give you the power to load a signed bill into a lemon, orange, or other fruit option completely undetected inches from the spectators' eyes. It's as fast as a rattlesnake bite and just as deadly.

I'm not crazy about the image—rattlesnakes are not my idea of a good time—but it does convey speed.

The copy goes on from there, explaining more about the effect.

Why so much copy? Well, this magic trick sells for four hundred dollars. Yes, $400. (If you want it—I believe they have one and only one left—see http://www.dennymagic.com). As you'll see later in this book, one of my secret principles is: *The higher the cost, the more copy you'll need.*

Again, magic catalogs can be a great resource for learning hypnotic copy. They teach you to focus on *what people get.* Whenever you write copy, ask yourself, "What does the reader want?" Focus on giving *that* to them.

But before we go much deeper into copywriting, let's peek behind the door that says HYPNOSIS on it.

15

WHAT IS HYPNOSIS?

Recently I interviewed Dan Kennedy, famous marketing consultant. During the course of our chat, Dan said, "You can't go very far in business without learning a little hypnosis."

I was surprised. Not because of the statement, but because of who said it. I never realized Dan knew the importance of hypnosis. The truth is, understanding hypnosis helps you understand the mind of your reader.

People are self-centered. That's not negative. That's reality. They walk around in their own trance. Their bundle of experiences, beliefs, thoughts, and actions create a unique world where they live, move, and breathe. Each of us, in short, is in a hypnotic state. We'll never admit it. But we're in it.

The first step in writing Hypnotic Copy is understanding the mind of your reader. That mind is *not* focused on your writing. That mind is absorbed with its own concerns. In order for you to make contact, you have to enter that mind where it already is.

All good hypnotists know this. In order for any hypnotist to lead you into a state of relaxed awareness—which is what hypnosis is— they have to meet you where you are mentally.

They have to make what's called "an agreement" with you: You agree that the hypnotist can relax you, and the hypnotist can then do it. Without this unspoken agreement, hypnosis is not likely to happen.

Famous copywriter Robert Collier said you had to meet the reader where their thoughts already are. You can do this with a headline that speaks to their problem, or to their dream. What you need to do is begin your letter where the prospect already is in his own head. This is a way to create agreement with your reader. It's a way to build rapport.

Collier wrote, "Your problem, then, is to find a point of contact with his (the reader's) interests, his desires, some feature that will flag his attention and make your letter stand out from all the others the moment he reads the first line."

Again, this will become clearer as you go through this book. For now, I want you to realize that the more you can meet your reader on the mental level where they are already preoccupied, the more you can create Hypnotic Writing that moves them to where you want them to be: into a *buying trance*.

But before I explain how to persuade people through your words, let's stop and take a look at a formula or two for persuasion and influence.

16

TWO WAYS TO CAUSE ACTION

As you probably already know, there are two ways to cause people to take action. One is pain and the other is pleasure.

These are known throughout history. They are the two primary human activators. In short, you can get people to move with a board smacked across their butt or a juicy carrot dangling in front of their face.

Most people in marketing and psychology agree that the first motivator—pain—is more powerful than the second. While I agree, I think that is a disservice to humankind.

Why add to the misery in the world? I say let's make a difference and focus on pleasure. Let's make people happy. I think that is a sounder way to help people, as well as to help you.

Can you imagine how wonderful life will be for all of us if we focused on our wants—our desires, our pleasures, our goals—and not on our pains?

But let's start with the basic formula for persuading people, which traditionally includes the pain motivator. Starting here will give you a better sense of how to use my revised system later, which I explain in a moment.

This strategy is probably 2,500 years old and goes back to Aristotle and the ancient Greeks. The great orators of that time spoke to persuade people. Aristotle gave them a formula for doing just that.

Here it is:

1. *Exordium.* Make a shocking statement or tell a story to get attention.
2. *Narratio.* Pose the problem the reader/listener is having.
3. *Confirmation.* Offer a solution to the problem.
4. *Peroratio.* State the benefits of action on the solution.

This should look a little familiar to you. It's very similar to the classic advertising formula known as *AIDA: Attention, Interest, Desire, Action.*

Because of both of those formulas, most of my sales oriented writing follows along the easy path of answering these questions:

1. Are you getting attention with your opening?
2. Are you stating a problem the reader cares about?
3. Are you offering a solution that really works?
4. Are you asking the reader to take action?

In short, and in a very simplified version, here is Aristotle's formula in modern dress:

1. Problem
2. Promise
3. Proof
4. Price

Not much to it, is there?

Let's look at each step and see what secrets it holds.

PROBLEM

Begin your writing with a headline that calls out the audience you want by focusing on their problem. For example, if you sell something to cure, say "heel spurs," then use a headline such as

Got heel spurs?

Or say you are selling a weight loss product of some sort. You might use a headline such as

Want to lose weight?

What you are doing is rounding up the people who will want to buy from you by focusing on their problem or issue.

Again, say you are a massage therapist with your own site. Your headline at the top of your website might be

Stressed? Want to release your tension in 30 minutes or less?

By now you should grasp what I'm doing here. I'm simply asking myself, "What is the problem my visitors are having?" Whatever it is, I create a lead headline at the top of my web site that speaks to it.

That's step one: focusing on the problem.

PROMISE

You got their attention with step one. Now mention your promise. Using the "heel spurs" headline from earlier, a follow-through might be

New herbs reduce or remove heel spurs in 30 days.

And the second example on losing weight, might read

New nondiet approach relies on your mind, not your food, to lose weight fast.

And the massage therapist example might read

My hands have eased 3,500 bodies just like yours. I can help you, too.

As you can probably gather, what you are doing in this second step is explaining how you solve the problem mentioned in the first step. This will keep people reading. If you are truly focused on their problem, you will be putting them into a waking trance with Hypnotic Writing.

PROOF

Next, you need proof. We live in the age of skepticism. People are used to going to web sites and hearing wild or unsubstantiated claims. Their guard is up. Not only that, but the Federal Trade Commission (FTC) is watching you. They want proof, too, that you can deliver. So step three in my formula is to focus on your proof, or your evidence. These can be in the form of a guarantee, testimonials, or anything else you can think of to convince people you are being honest with them. Examples might be

Your heel spurs will disappear in 30 days or you can have all your money back.
11,500 people healed of heel spurs so far.
Research shows people lose an average of 33 pounds with this new plan.
You will feel so relaxed from my massage that you will fall asleep on my table.

And so it goes. Again, what you are doing is proving your promise. This is where you bring in your evidence that your promise will work.

PRICE

Finally, you need to ask for what you want. If you want people to sign up for your newsletter, say so. If you want them to buy your product, say so. If you want them to call you, say so. People want to be led. But they won't take action unless you spell it out for them, and tell them the price for doing so. Examples might be

If you don't take care of those heel spurs today, where will you be tomorrow?
Order our special herbs right now for only $19.95.

MY UPDATED FORMULA

Philosopher Vernon Howard once said, "If we believe in the necessity of trying to win over others, we will also believe in the need for wearisome scheming."

Let's not scheme. Let's not try to win people over with our interests in mind. Instead, let's focus on what *they* want. Let's focus on their pleasure, not their pain. The more you can deliver the good that people long for, the more people will be almost hypnotically drawn to you and your writing.

Remember, I said I don't think we need to add to the bleakness of the world. So I am bold and say let's delete step one altogether. If you focus on pain, you surely get people's attention. You are speaking to their greatest concern.

Have you noticed how often ads on television and in newspapers focus on pain to get your attention? The method works. But I don't want to add to the pain in the world. Since a basic truth in psychology is that people get more of whatever they focus on, I don't even want to mention their pain.

There's an article on my web site at www.mrfire.com about this whole subject. I reproduce it here because it so relevant.

The Greatest Motivator Isn't What You Think

or

What I Learned from Drew Barrymore and Adam Sandler on Valentine's Day
Joe Vitale
www.mrfire.com

It's Valentine's Day as I write this. Nerissa and I just returned from watching the new movie *50 First Dates* starring the beautiful Drew Barrymore and the funny Adam Sandler. Besides being a hilarious movie in a beautiful setting with a heartfelt message of true love, it also caused me to have an "aha" right in the middle of it.

Somewhere around halfway through the movie, as Adam is again reminding short-term memory loss victim Drew that he loves her, I suddenly realized the power of the greatest motivator of all time.

But let me first set the stage.

Most psychologists, direct marketers, and anyone who persuades for a living will tell you there are only two basic motivators: pain or pleasure. You either go toward what you want or away from what you don't want.

The standard argument is that pain is more powerful. I've tended to agree but also have stated I would not focus on pain for idealistic reasons. I simply don't want to spread pain in the world. Focusing on it causes you to feel it. I don't want to contribute to the misery many feel. So my stance has been to focus on pleasure as a motivator in my sales letters and web sites.

Most marketing experts agree that pain is the best trigger to focus on in any ad or sales campaign.

They love to find a prospect's basic problem and then rub their noses in it. They figure the pain would make the person buy or change.

The most common example they give is the insurance salesperson who tries to sell you home coverage. If he focuses on pleasure, you will put off buying. If he tells you your house is on fire, you will buy. Pain causes immediate action.

So, like everyone else, I "knew" pain was the greater motivator. I simply focused on pleasure because it is a more noble route.

But then I saw Drew Barrymore and Adam Sandler in their new movie and suddenly I felt awakened, energized, and validated.

Here's the film's plot in a nutshell:

Adam is in love with a woman who can't remember anything from the day before, due to a head injury in an auto accident the year before. Every day is a new day. And every day Adam has to win her over again. Every date is new. Hence the title *50 First Dates*.

At one point in it, as Adam is again wooing Drew, I suddenly realized what I was really seeing.

I saw that pleasure was the greatest motivator of all.

Adam is pursuing Drew every day, despite the pain and the

odds, because of his growing love for her. He is going after pleasure. The pleasure goal is so powerful it erases every pain he might experience.

In short, all the marketing experts who say pain is the greatest motivator have forgotten the power of our driving force in life: love.

People will scale mountains with luggage on their backs, swim upstream in a hurricane, and battle armies and all odds in order to fulfill that hardwired emotion in us to love and be loved. Love rules.

All the examples we were given were unfair. Someone trying to sell insurance and resorting to pain hasn't figured out the real pleasure button to make someone buy. They've been too lazy to search for the pleasure trigger. Focusing on pain was simply an easy cop-out, a handy approach.

It's the same with all the massive ad campaigns that fail. Trying to get someone to quit smoking or stop drugs because of the pain they depict in the ad is the wrong approach. If we suddenly focused on the pleasure someone would have when they stopped smoking or taking drugs, we'd be moving in the right direction.

This is obvious to me after watching the movie.

Our goal as marketing and businesspeople isn't to tell people what's wrong with them or to remind them of their pain, but to help them imagine and then experience the pleasure they long to have.

It's noble, yes, *and* it works.

Love moves everyone.

Love is the great motivator.

Love is the great pleasure trigger.

According to my friend Kevin Hogan, author of *The Psychology of Persuasion*, love isn't an emotion but a mind-set. And as a mind-set, it is actually stronger than any emotion.

In short, you're dealing with the most powerful motivator of all time.

Reveal what there is to love about your product or service

and you'll give people authentic reasons to do business with you. Call it Love-Based Marketing. You won't sell everyone with it. You'll sell only those who are a match for your offer. That, in the end, is all you want. Then you're happy and so are your customers.

Just like Drew Barrymore and Adam Sandler, you'll find a match to write home about.

And you might make a little money along the way, to boot.

I have to confess that since writing this article, my thoughts have changed a little. For example, I think that gently reminding people of the pain they are in may be a wise and even loving thing to do. After all, if they are suffering and are in denial about it, a little Zen whack may be in order.

I also know that sometimes you want to mention the pain upfront because that is where the person's mind is. In other words, keeping Collier's advice in mind, if someone has sore feet, the best headline of all for them may very well be **Sore Feet?**.

I would still want to test that headline against one based on pleasure, such as **Want Foot Relief?** or **At Last—No More Foot Aches!**

The point is, I want to focus on the positive for idealist reasons, but I'm enough of a realist to know sometimes people need to be reminded of their pain in order to nudge them in the direction of their pleasure.

Eugene Schwartz, one of the greatest copywriters of all time, wrote in his famous book, *Breakthrough Advertising*:

"A copy writer's first qualifications are imagination and enthusiasm. You are literally the script writer for your prospect's dreams. You are the chronicler of his future. Your job is to show him in minute detail all the tomorrows that your product makes possible for him."

Ah, yes!

Show your reader his or her dreams.

"You are literally the script writer for your prospect's dreams."

That's focusing on the positive.

MOTIVATION WITHOUT PAIN

So let's try creating a basic hypnotic message with just the other three steps:

1. Promise
2. Proof
3. Price

Here's how it might work.

Promise

In step one, you round up your audience by focusing on what they want. An example might be

Want to play the guitar fast and easy?

Proof

You then go to step two and offer proof. An example might be

Amy's Stripped-Down Guitar Method promises to teach you how to play your favorite song in one weekend flat

Price

Finally, in step three, you ask for their order by mentioning the price.

For only $19.99, you can be playing the guitar at the end of this weekend. Just click here

There you have it. You created a basic hypnotically written message and didn't cause people to feel bad at all. Your final piece of writing might look like this:

Want to play the guitar in one weekend flat? Amy's Stripped-Down Guitar Method e-book shows anyone how

to do it, guaranteed or your money back. Click here to pay $19.99 and download it right now

Not bad for a few minutes' work. But is that good enough? And how do you apply this to your web site, anyway?

Just keep reading.

17

WHAT ABOUT YOUR WEB SITE?

You're intelligent enough to know that the formula mentioned earlier will help you easily create a short piece of very simple Hypnotic Writing. That might be fine for an ad. Or even a post-card, telegram, or, of course, an e-mail. But what about a full-scale web site? How do you apply my three-step hypnotic formula to create your own hypnotically written web site?

The answer should seem obvious. It's certainly simple. All you do is expand on each of the three steps in my peace-loving formula. In other words:

1. *Promise.* Your headline can be short and sweet. But why not a secondary headline under it? That works, too.
2. *Proof.* Your proof can be testimonials, a guarantee, scientific studies, quotes from authorities, a statistic, or anything else that helps convince people of your promise.
3. *Price.* Your call to action can be several reminders to buy now, as well as how to buy, and where to buy now. You want people to act now, not tomorrow, so your price might include bonuses for acting right this minute. "Order now and get three e-books for free."

You can see an example of how the three steps have been used to create a full-blown web site at http://www.strippeddownguitar.com/.

I'm using it as a model as I know the author of the site and helped her create it. If you look at the site closely, you'll find she uses longer copy to expand on each of the three points in my formula. Here are some excerpts right now, in case you can't get to her site at the moment. (See what follows.)

PROMISE

**How to play any song you love on the
guitar—in one weekend flat!**

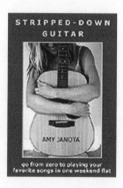

**Find out how to amaze your friends, your loved ones,
and most of all, YOURSELF by singing and playing
SONGS YOU LOVE in as little as one weekend—
even if you've never touched a guitar before,
are tone deaf, and suffer from major stage fright!**

PROOF

I promise, after just **one weekend with STRIPPED-DOWN GUITAR**, you will be inspired and thrilled with how satisfying the guitar can be! And once you've gotten a taste of **IMPRESSING**

your friends and family by performing your favorite songs, you will be **completely STOKED!**

Playing guitar **STRIPPED-DOWN style** is **CLEAR, CONCISE**, and geared to give you **QUICK RESULTS** that will keep you engaged and excited about your developing skills.

In **STRIPPED-DOWN GUITAR**, I reveal secrets like:

- My one-weekend, **step-by-step "stripped-down" method** to start playing the guitar.
- The **two guitar accessories** a beginner cannot do without.
- The best place to find the **chords to your favorite songs** on the Internet.
- The most important **secret to choosing your first song** to learn.
- Finger by finger instructions for **making the most common guitar chords**.
- The indispensable secret for actually **getting your fingers to learn faster**.
- The **number one thing you need to know about guitar tab sites** that I had to learn the VERY hard way.
- The most important technique for **freeing up space in your brain** to learn more quickly.
- The little-known fact that can make **a decent singer out of anyone** and the one secret that can have **you singing any song better** . . . instantly!
- The four indispensable **techniques for overcoming stage fright**.
- How to deal with an unsympathetic audience member.

—So you can capture the magic of being a musician, even if you never dreamed you could!

PRICE

Click to order STRIPPED-DOWN GUITAR now!

Your satisfaction is assured through our no-risk, you-can't-lose, 100%, no-questions-asked, ironclad money-back guarantee.

If for any reason, you aren't thrilled and satisfied with your purchase, just contact me directly within 30 days and I'll refund 100% of your purchase price.

What I'm saying is don't decide now if **STRIPPED-DOWN GUITAR** is right for you.

Try it out for one full month—risk free.

If it doesn't help you **overcome any stumbling blocks** to learning to play great songs on the guitar, if it doesn't **guide you step by step** through picking a song, learning it, and honing it for performance, if it doesn't **take you by the hand** and teach you exactly how to get your fingers working and how to get your voice out there—even if you've been labeled tone deaf or never thought you could play—if it doesn't make progress on guitar **easier than you ever dreamed possible**, and if it doesn't **inspire** you to keep on learning and playing, then I don't want your money and I'll gladly give it all back.

You have nothing to lose!

So, how much is this tremendous experience going to cost you? Well, the regular price for **STRIPPED-DOWN GUITAR** is $39.99. However, for a limited time, we are running an introductory offer and **you can have it at a discount** for only $19.99. **That's 50% off—but you must act now!**

Plus, because you *download* the course, you can have this information immediately, and get started learning to play the guitar **today!** And

It doesn't matter if it's 2 in the morning!

Click to order STRIPPED-DOWN GUITAR now!

Amy successfully covered all three steps in my formula—Promise, Proof, and Price—with words that are easy to read. If you are at all interested in learning how to play the guitar fast, you'll buy Amy's e-book.

But how much copy is too much?

18

How Long
Is Too Long?

By now you can see that you can make your web site or sales letter pretty lengthy just following the three-step, no-pain formula. This doesn't mean you want a web site or letter that runs on forever. But it does mean you can take your time to share your message. After all, people will read any amount of words on a web site, *as long as they are interesting to them*. And that's the trick that makes millionaires out of paupers.

Keep in mind that as a general rule, *the more you tell, the more you sell*. That means don't be afraid of long copy (*copy* means *words* in marketing lingo). Web sites with long copy (lots of words) tend to do better than web sites with fewer words. But again, they can't just be any words. As you know, if you bore people, they will leave your site in a nanosecond. Boredom breaks the trance.

My own rule of thumb is this: *The more money you are asking for, the more words you should write.*

If you are asking people to sign up for only a free newsletter, a few well chosen words may do. If you want them to buy something under ten dollars, again, a few well chosen words may be enough. But if you want someone to buy a $15,000 exercise machine—as the people over at http://www.QuickGym.com want you to do— you have a lot of explaining to do. That will take some words. They better be hypnotic words, too.

The point is, the length of copy at your web site will depend on what you are selling. If people are familiar with your product or service, you may not have to say much. If people easily understand why your price is what it is, again, you may not have to say much. But if you have to explain your product, or your price, do so with as many words as you need.

Your guiding principle should always be to focus on the interests of the people visiting your site or reading your sales letter. Again, people will read long copy—they read books, articles, and newspapers, for example—*as long as it is interesting to them*. If people aren't reading your web site copy, then you haven't written to *their* interests.

Let's take a closer look at how to interest people.

19

WHAT EVERY READER WANTS TO KNOW

Ready for some specific insights on how to create Hypnotic Writing?

If you give people what they want, they'll listen to you. What does every reader want in your writing? That's hard to say, because everything you write is different. But people generally ask themselves a few questions when they pick up something to read. Here they are:

"Who cares?"
"So what?"
"What's in it for me?"

Imagine Bart Simpson, the animated loser of television fame, asking those questions of you. Readers are more polite, but the questions are there, lurking in the backs of their minds. Address those questions if you want to create Hypnotic Writing.

I learned about those questions while educating myself to be a speaker. They are the same questions every audience asks, if only unconsciously. When you think about it, readers are looking over your writing for *their* reasons, not yours. They don't care what you want. They care about what *they* want. Every reader, every audience, is the same.

You need to know the answers to Bart's questions. What *is* in it for the reader? What are his benefits? What will he get out of it? Why *should* he care about what you've written? The bottom line is "*so what?*"

Can you provide answers? If you can't, your readers—well, you won't have *any* readers.

Think about it. When you pick up a magazine, or even your mail, you go through it and weed out what you don't want. If the article or the letter doesn't grab you in some way, you go right by it. Right? You don't read every article in your favorite magazine, do you? You might glance at it and as soon as you see it's not for you, you flip the pages.

Your readers will do the same thing to your writing. You better capture their attention *immediately*. How?

By thinking of what they want. Again, look at Bart's questions:

"Who cares?" (Well, who *does* care about your writing? Why should they care?)

"So what?" (Well, *so what*? Why does your writing matter? Do you have something important to say? Is it *really* important?)

"What's in it for me?" (Well, what *is* in it for him? What will he get out of your writing or your offer?)

You have to put your feet into the other person's shoes. Imagine what they want. Rapport is a key to any success in selling. It's a key to Hypnotic Writing, too. When you understand what your readers care about, you are in a position of power. You can then create something that will grab them where they live (so to speak, of course).

A manager may be interested in motivation. An accountant may be interested in tax savings. A writer may want easier ways to write (hence my strong headline in my letter selling Thoughtline).

Get out of your own ego and into your readers'. Don't give them what you want; give them what *they* want. Or, if you're offering something new, tell them about it in a way that appeals to *them*, not you. When Disney Studios released the movie *Arachnophobia*, it was billed as a comedy–thriller. When they discovered that audiences didn't care about comedy–thrillers, they billed the movie as a horror picture. Same movie, different approach. You have to think of your readers, not yourself.

One of the reasons Robert Collier's letters were so successful is because he merged with his readers. He began his letters from *their* viewpoint. Though Collier wanted people to order his products, his letters were friendly and personal and began by meeting the reader right where their mind was.

It's also a principle of Aikido, the martial art from Japan. Rather than beating someone into agreeing with you (as some politicians do with their advertising), Aikido says take people from where they already are to where you want them to be. Use their own momentum but redirect it. In other words, when writing a letter to get a point across, don't just whack the reader with your point. That's blunt. Instead, begin the letter from where the reader is, maybe by agreeing with him on some issue, and *then* move the letter in the direction of what you want to say.

Your reader is selfish. All he cares about is himself. Appeal to that interest. I often get query letters from authors who want me to consider publishing their books. Far too often the letter is about them and what they want, rarely about what I may want. You know what I do with those letters, don't you? (Take a guess.) If you just take a little time to consider your reader, you'll begin the process of writing something that will hypnotize him.

Consider this: If a woman knocked on your door right now and offered to help you write Hypnotic Writing, you'd listen, wouldn't you? But what if the same woman wanted to sell you diapers? The first one appeals to what *you* want, the second to what *she* wants. Which lady will hold your attention?

Or consider this: If you were a part of a group photo shooting and later were handed the photo, whose face would you look for first? Obviously, your own. That's because you interests you. Same goes for your readers: They are interested in themselves, not you.

Remember Bart Simpson's questions: "So what? Who cares? What's in it for me?" and *answer* them *before* you start writing. Consider this step part of your research phase (step two in turbocharging your writing). It's an essential step in creating writing that will nail your reader's eyes to the page.

That's what you want, isn't it?

20

THE HYPNOTIC POWER OF REPETITION

SCENE ONE

In the movie, *Good Will Hunting*, the counselor, played by Robin Williams, lovingly confronts the disturbed young man in his office with the phrase, "It's not your fault."

After a pause, Williams again says, "It's not your fault."

After yet another pause, he again says, "It's not your fault."

By the time the scene is over, the young man breaks down and cries. The counselor and patient hug. A transformation has occurred. It's a powerful moment in the film.   It's unforgettable.

And it's hypnotic.

Why?

SCENE TWO

My girlfriend and I are having dinner. We have gone out to see a movie. Afterwards we drive through the city night, the top down on my new BMW Z3, as we hold hands and breathe the fresh, cool air. Now, at dinner, we are feeling deeply close.

At that moment by girlfriend leans over to me, looks me right in the eye, and asks, "Do you know I love you?"

I quickly nod and smile. Yes, of course, I know she loves me.

She doesn't blink an eye. She again looks at me and says, "Do you know I love you?"

I laugh a little nervously. "Yes, I know it," I reply.

She doesn't stop. She again says, "Do you know I love you?"

I'm silent this time. Now I'm *really* hearing her.

Suddenly my heart wells up with emotion. I feel an overwhelming amount of love in my chest. I look at my girlfriend and realize—truly *get*—that she loves me. It's a moment I'll never forget.

It, too, is hypnotic.

Why?

I've discovered that one of the most powerful tools of persuasion any hypnotic writer can have is simply this: repetition.

Don't dismiss this concept. It helped Robin Williams heal a troubled youth. It helped my girlfriend get into my heart. And it can help you influence your readers to do what you want.

Repetition isn't new, of course. P.T. Barnum, maybe the best marketing mind the world has ever seen, used this concept back in the late 1800s. As I point out in my book on Barnum, *There's A Customer Born Every Minute*, one of his ads had one line repeating:

Two Living Whales
Two Living Whales
Two Living Whales
Two Living Whales
Two Living Whales

You can't help but take a quick look at Barnum's ad and know he has two living whales on display.

Advertising man and author Kenneth Goode, in his 1932 book, *Advertising*, wrote "As a matter of fact, the greatest of all advertising tricks is that of persistently pounding away at the same suggestion while still keeping the appearance of freshness of idea."

And Walter Honek, a mail-order genius who wrote the 1994 book, *My Amazing Discovery*, said: "Do not hesitate to repeat key words and phrases. Repeat them as often as necessary."

Repetition is hypnotic. It's what good hypnotists use to install their suggestions in your mind. Their repeatedly saying, "You are getting sleepy" is said because, heard enough times, you *will* get sleepy.

The same thing can happen in your writing. Consciously choose to repeat your main points. Don't be afraid to re-say something. The more you repeat your basic offer or basic reasons to buy, the more you will influence the reader's unconscious mind.

Repetition is hypnotic.

Repetition is hypnotic.

Repetition is hypnotic.

Just ask Robin Williams.

Or my girlfriend.

21

THE INNER GAME OF HYPNOTIC WRITING

"There is an inner game of EVERYTHING," said W. Timothy Gallwey. He should know. Gallwey has written several books on "inner game" playing. The most popular are *The Inner Game of Tennis*, *The Inner Game of Golf*, and *The Inner Game of Skiing*. My personal favorite is the one he co-authored with Barry Green, *The Inner Game of Music*.

There's an inner game of writing, too, and it plays a major role in developing Hypnotic Writing. Let me prove it to you by applying the inner game principles to writing.

SELF ONE: THE CRITIC

When you're writing, have you noticed a little voice in your head judging your work? You might even hear it right now. It's the voice talking about what you're reading as you are reading. It's the voice that tells you that your writing is good or lousy (usually the latter). You may be so used to this well-intended unseen companion that you don't know he's there in your head. But he's there. Believe me. And it is this inner critic called Self One in the inner game that stops you from writing with ease, flow, and originality.

If you find a part of you saying things like, "You aren't a good writer," or, "Watch your spelling!" then you've heard Self One. In my first book, *Zen and the Art of Writing*, I called this voice Mr. Editor.

Our educational system installed this internal editor when we were kids in English class. You and I were taught to watch our spelling, grammar, punctuation, logic, sentence structure, and so on. We were made so cautious of mistakes that we actually became *paranoid*. We made Mr. Editor our trusted friend and advisor and let him run the show whenever we picked up a pen to write.

But Self One isn't such a good buddy. It's this very voice that prevents you from writing some topnotch material. Though Mr. Editor seems like he is helping you, he is actually keeping you protected. Safe. Controlled. And under those circumstances, you can't be free to write anything that will grab attention.

Imagine this: You are about to write a letter. You sit down, flip on the computer, and prepare to tap the keys. But suddenly your sixth grade English teacher appears at your side! Oh no! "What are you writing?" your teacher asks. "A letter," you say. "Let me help," he says. Gulp. As you begin to write, your teacher judges your work. "Did you spell that right?" he asks. "That line doesn't make sense," he says.

Do you think you would get very far under those circumstances? Yet that very teacher is in your head, whispering in your ear, as you write! No wonder most of us create mediocre work! We're under guard!

In my writing classes I watch people write. I see them write a line, stop, think it over, scratch it out, write another, and try again. That's stuttering on paper! Those students are listening to their internal editors and it's blocking them! Mark Twain was right. Imagine what the world would sound like if you and I edited ourselves so ruthlessly when we spoke!

Another exercise to reveal your internal critic is something I do in my workshops. I have people pair off. One stands, the other sits. The one sitting begins to write something, anything. The one standing gently, quietly, but persistently, judges what is being written. No one can write under those circumstances.

It's too distracting. Yet we do this to ourselves every time we sit to write!

It's time for a change.

SELF TWO: THE MASTER WRITER

Also within you is a wiser part called Self Two, the Master.

Right now you are reading these lines and maybe you're aware of your thoughts as you read. But it isn't quite that simple, is it? Going on automatically and unconsciously is a complex system of body–mind coordination. Not only are you looking at these words with eyes that are constantly moving, which have muscles operating them that you aren't aware of, but you are also receiving this input from a brain that is firing off neurons in more directions than either of us can imagine. And even as you read, your body is somehow breathing, your heart is pumping, your cells are renewing, and much more. If you suddenly put all of the actions under the control of Self One, you'd probably die.

In short, there is a part of you that can handle major life and death duties. It's Self Two. And this very same part of you can help you compose Hypnotic Writing!

Sound incredible? If so, that's Self One, the doubting Thomas, gagging on the idea of giving up control.

I first experienced the incredible freedom of Self Two writing while at the Option Institute in Sheffield, Massachusetts. I was there to spend a week with Barry Neil Kaufman, author of *Son-Rise, Giant Steps, To Love Is to Be Happy With*, and several other popular books (all worth reading, by the way).

Each night I would sit at my little desk and record my experiences. Occasionally Self One (the Editor, remember) would whisper in my ear, "Your writing isn't going well, is it?"

But I was relaxed and happy and content to *allow* myself the freedom to write whatever I wanted. Rather than forcing myself to edit my work as I wrote it, I decided to simply enjoy writing. I let go. And "something else" began to write.

Now this "something else" isn't anything metaphysical. It's simply a wise part of you. When you get out of the way, "it" is there.

The writing happens naturally. Think back to the last conversation you had with someone you liked and felt comfortable with. Didn't you just *say* the words as they came to you? You didn't think out or plan what you were going to say. You trusted yourself to speak. And you did.

You've written a lot of material in your life, haven't you? You've read a lot of books on writing, and you've read many other books on a wide variety of subjects, right? You've also gone to school, maybe even to college, and you've had many, many (too many?) hours of writing instruction.

You haven't forgotten any of it! It's all in you right now. Self Two, the Master Writer, has absorbed everything. If you let that part of you come out and write, you'll be surprised at the results!

You might even be *hypnotized* by them!

THREE STEPS TO INNER WRITING

Here are the three steps to the "inner game" of Hypnotic Writing:

1. Step One: Set a goal.
2. Step Two: Be aware of the moment.
3. Step Three: Trust what happens.

Let's take it a step at a time.

Step One: Set a Goal

Before you write, set a goal (sound familiar?). Decide on what you want from your writing. Do you want to write a story? A letter? An article? A book chapter? A script? It doesn't matter. Just select your goal.

Gallwey suggests you enrich your inner game experience by making a three-part goal. This is his way of helping you make your goal *concrete*. He suggests you ask yourself these questions:

- "What do I want for *performance*?"
  Example: To create a powerful sales letter.
- "What do I want for *experience*?"
  Example: To enjoy the process of writing.

* "What do I want to *learn*?"

Example: To write without Self One interrupting.

Answering those questions will give you a complete target to hand over to Self Two, the Master Writer within you. By describing your goal completely, you will be putting your order in and making Self Two aware of what you want.

You're making a request. You're asking Self Two to help you create a specific piece of writing. In order to get what you want, you must *know* what you want. So be sure your goal is exact, specific, and tangible. If you don't have a clear goal, you won't get a clear or useful result.

Self Two takes orders. Your job in this step is to give it a clear request.

Step Two: Be Aware of the Moment

All you have is *this* moment. The past is gone and the future isn't here yet. Thoughts of the past happen in *this* moment. Visions of the future happen in *this* moment. Your point of power is *now*.

This is the secret to keeping Self One, the chatterbox "monkey mind," quiet. When you are focused on this moment, you squelch Mr. Editor. Eastern philosophers have known this for centuries. Be aware of something in this moment, something that occupies your mind, and you concentrate all your attention on the moment at hand.

Gallwey suggests tennis players pay close attention to the ball, to see its color, seams, movement. What I do in writing is focus on the pen moving across the page, or on my fingers hitting the keyboard (I have to see the keys to know what to hit). Though I can still hear Self One muttering, I ignore him. In a very real way I am in a hypnotic trance as I write, what horror-king Stephen King calls "the writer's trance."

When you're focused on the activity happening right now, you are open to Self Two's guiding hand and not vulnerable to Self One's editorial voice. If you use a word processor or computer, turn your screen *off*. Just concentrate on the writing. Without the screen your mind won't be able to edit your work. (Some new software comes with a built-in program to prevent you from seeing the screen as you write. See www.HypnoticWriting Wizard.com)

Step Three: Trust What Happens

Everything in life is—or can be—a learning experience. Even if you don't write the draft you think you want to write, you will write *something*. And you will learn something in the process. Accept that.

Trusting Self Two, the Master Writer, means being willing to experiment. By letting the Master Writer within you come through and direct, or influence, your writing you will be giving yourself the opportunity to learn, to grow, to expand, and to enrich your writing.

Trust the inner game approach to writing. *Allow* words to flow through you. Don't edit them. You've set your goal. You've focused on something in the moment to keep the editor inside quiet. And you wrote something as a result—probably something surprising and maybe even spectacular. Self Two came through!

Self Two probably already helps you in your writing. Whenever you think you want to write a larger work, say a novel, you usually have a sense of the whole project. You don't have the *complete* idea in your mind, only a sense that it will be a novel. Well, how do you know it's a novel and not a short story? Somehow your feeling— where is *it* coming from?—lets you know your idea is going to be a book. You haven't begun the book and haven't even thought much about it. But it feels like a novel and not a story.

Whom are you trusting? What part of you is telling you, "This is a book!"? Isn't it the Master Writer within you?

If you have difficulty playing the inner game of Hypnotic Writing, it is because your inner editor, nasty old Self One, has a tight grip on your mind. That's okay. You're not doomed. There's hope!

You can try doodling for awhile before writing. Or put on some meditative background music, something gentle and soothing like Baroque music (*not* the Rolling Stones!). Or try freewriting for a while to loosen up. Runners stretch before a race. You can warm up with a few minutes of undirected, spontaneous writing. Another idea is to distract yourself completely before writing. That is, go mow the lawn or work out and then come back to your work. I often take a break by playing my harmonica or working on a new song (I prefer it to working out).

Some writers *enjoy* struggling with their writing. Why? Because they come from the "no pain, no gain" mentality. Some tennis players, for example, after experiencing the ease of letting their Self Two help them play tennis, *still* go out on the court and fight to improve themselves. It's an ego trip, my friend. As Gallwey wrote in *The Inner Game of Tennis*, "You feel that *you* are in control, that *you* are the master of the situation." Hah!

When you continue to struggle to write (or play tennis), you feel a sense of satisfaction. Maybe even dissatisfaction. But—and this is the main point—*you* are still there. Still involved, still controlling, still trying to direct the show. If that describes you, then you have identified with Self One, the critic.

Though it's not an immediate ego gratifier, it's wiser to give in to Self Two, the Master. If that bothers you, then consider this: After you have written something based on these principles, *you can take the credit for it!*

You don't have to tell anyone that Self Two helped you write that best selling book or award winning script. No one has to know. *No One!* So feel free to play the inner game to writing. Set a clear goal, focus on something in the moment, and trust what happens. Later on, edit your work, perfect it, and *take credit for it!*

After all, my friend, *you* did the writing, didn't you?

22

IMITATION SUGAR IS SWEET, TOO!

Imitation isn't only the sincerest form of flattery; it's also a powerful way to quickly learn new writing skills.

Mark Twain learned how to write by imitating other writers. The great author, as a youth, used to set newspaper stories in type. This tedious printing process gave Twain the chance to imitate writers. As he slowly copied their stories, he became aware of the fundamentals of fine writing.

Steve Allen, the radio and television celebrity, learned how to write humor by copying jokes. Allen would go to the library, borrow some joke books, and then copy all of the jokes onto index cards. Because Allen had to copy each word by hand, he, like Twain, learned the subtle inner formula for writing.

How does imitation work such wonders? Easy. You probably drive a lot. Have you ever walked down a street you normally drive? Did you notice that you saw, heard, and learned a lot more about the street when you were on foot? When you slow down, you pay attention to all the wonderful things you normally miss. The same thing happens when you copy the greats. You suddenly become aware of what you normally never hear or see.

I tell people in my writing classes to take a story they love and copy it word for word. This exercise gives them the same experience

Mark Twain and Steve Allen got. By imitating great writing, you learn how to create great writing. It gives you something close to the same feelings the author probably had when he wrote the story. That's powerful.

You can imitate anyone in order to learn new skills. I've taught harmonica players to imitate great players by slowing down the recordings and copying each note they hear. And when I was 16 and wanted to be a writer, I imitated Jack London and William Saroyan until I understood how they wrote their masterpieces.

Reading and copying great writing is comparable to what an athlete does when he watches videos of other athletes. A skier watches expert skiers handle tough slopes; tennis players watch films of tennis champions; swimmers watch videos of legendary swimmers. All of these people are training their minds (and bodies) to record the pattern for creating success.

Writers can't watch videos of other writers and pick up what the authors are doing because writing is largely an internal experience. But if you pick up a piece of writing, something created by a master writer, and copy it, word for word, you begin to internalize the subtle intricacies used to create that writing.

Imitation isn't stealing (unless you try to sell the imitation). It's learning.

What I want you to do now is train your mind to create Hypnotic Writing. How? First, you have to find some Hypnotic Writing. Look around your room. What are the articles, letters, or books that have stuck with you over the years? What have you read recently that you could not forget? You might have read a novel, a short story, a letter, a direct mail advertisement, and even a memo. Collect examples of writing that you regard as *hypnotic*. Since this is a subjective judgment, there aren't any wrong examples. Just gather examples of writing that you think is excellent.

Now select something from your pile of examples. Anything. Now write out the example. That is to say, take out a pad of paper and a pen and actually copy, word for word, the example in front of you. Simply reproduce it in your own handwriting.

Yes, this will take a couple of minutes. But it is a *priceless education*! You will learn more about the delicate inner workings of writing than you ever imagined. In the same way Mark Twain learned about writing by setting stories in type, and Steve Allen learned about jokes by copying them from library books, *you* will learn how to write material that is *unforgettable*.

Look at the bright side of this exercise: It's *free*!

And to help you along, here's my famous letter on Thoughtline. It's considered Hypnotic Writing at its best. Later on you'll get to analyze this letter, but for now, just copy it in your own handwriting.

Exercise: Copy this letter in your own handwriting.

I've Finally Found the Secret to Make Writing Easy!

It's called Thoughtline and you better hang on to your hat because this new software program is *awesome*!

Imagine Socrates helping you with your next writing. After an exciting series of questions, Socrates hands you a rough draft of your article. You then use Socrates' outline to guide your writing. Before you know it, you're done!

This isn't fantasy. Thoughtline is a breakthrough "artificial intelligence" program designed to ask mind-stretching questions. But that's not all. Thoughtline then takes your answers and organizes them into a logical outline! With the outline in hand, you know where you are going. You no longer have to face that agonizing blank page.

The first time I used Thoughtline I was *amazed* at what happened. It asked me deep, probing questions, gathered my answers, looked them over, sorted them, and then developed an outline for me that made my eyes pop. I actually *ran* into the other room to show my wife what Thoughtline had created!

Would *you* like to have a "secret friend" help you create irresistible letters, articles, books, and presentations?

Thoughtline is now my writing companion. I use it to think through projects, develop rough drafts, brainstorm new ideas, and much more. Thoughtline has saved me time, effort, and money. When an idea I had wasn't sound, Thoughtline told me so. When I need help fast, Thoughtline is there.

With Thoughtline I have literally become *more effective, intelligent, powerful, and prolific!*

One friend of mine, a speaker, is going out to buy a computer just so she can use Thoughtline to help her develop talks that will make her audience sit up and take notice. Clearly she can see how valuable this is!

Can you imagine what you could write with Thoughtline at your fingertips?

This is the *only* program I endorse because it is the only writing tool that *works!* (Isn't that what counts?)

Mark Twain wrote, "A man's intellect is stored powder; it cannot touch itself off; the fire must come from outside." Thoughtline is the "fire" you need to make your mind *explode!*

You can now benefit from this "talking" program, too. Though it retails for $295, you can now get Thoughtline for only $169. (You *save over $125!*) And that includes all the disks, a great manual, postage and handling, attractive case and technical support (though you won't need the latter as the program is *simple* to run).

Just think: The amount of new material you write with Thoughtline will probably more than pay for the package!

You'll be writing everything you've ever dreamed of (and more) only moments after you ask Thoughtline for help!

But *don't* take my word for it. See for yourself. Just fill out the enclosed form and mail it with your check.

Then stand back. Your computer will soon come *alive!*

Sincerely,

Joe Vitale

Author, *Turbocharge Your Writing*

Author, *Zen and the Art of Writing*

Co-author, *The Joy of Service!*

Award-Winning Journalist

P.S. If you don't send in your order I'll assume you don't have an IBM (or 100% compatible) computer with a hard drive. Because I know you would *buy this program* if you did! What person seeking breakthrough effectiveness in their writing wouldn't *buy this program*?!

P.P.S. Look. There's some writing you want to do but haven't started. Why wait any longer?

You have just fed your mind information on how to create Hypnotic Writing.

The more you read powerful writing, and the more you copy it out in your own hand, the more you will train your mind to write irresistible material. You can't do this exercise once and forget about it, however. Learning is eternal. You might want to set aside a time period every week so you can do nothing but teach your mind through the awesome power of imitation.

Sound too simple for you? Then keep one thing in mind: This one step could *transform* your entire ability to write material that walks, talks, and breathes!

If you want to know how to create Hypnotic Writing, then imitate people who are already doing it. When you copy their work, you begin to recognize how—and why—they got the results they achieved.

In the same way modeling a tennis player's form will help you become a better tennis player, imitating an excellent writer will teach you the form for excellent writing.

But don't take my word for it. Give the process a shot. Pick an example of terrific writing and write it out. You'll be amazed at what you will learn!

23

How to Jump-Start the Muse

Do you wait for inspiration before writing? Some writers do. Most of the people who sign up for my writing classes are looking for a shortcut to igniting the inner flames of inspiration. Though I offer some tips, I'm basically against it.

Why? Think back to the last job you had (or even your current one). Did you go to work only when inspiration hit? I doubt it. You went to work because you had to, because you wouldn't get paid if you didn't go. It's true for writing, too. Jack London advised writers to go after the muse with a club, not to sit around waiting for it to knock on your mental door. I wouldn't be that violent about it, but I think old Jack was on the right track.

My experience has been this: Start writing and the muse will come to you. Somehow the princess of creativity gets a whiff of your work, follows the scent, and ends up on your shoulder.

But she appears only after *you* take the first step. Here are five suggestions to help you take the first step, and to keep going once you've started the process.

1. *Just begin*. Put your pen to the paper and *move!* Write anything. *Anything!* Minister Eric Butterworth used to say he

was able to write so many books, columns, sermons, and radio shows because he began each day writing gibberish. Sci-Fi master Ray Bradbury free-associates on paper each morning until an idea clicks. Write whatever comes to mind. Sooner or later you'll stumble across a rich vein and you're off and running. Gibberish will turn into wisdom, free association into a mesmerizing story. Who knows?

2. *Don't edit!* Turn off your computer screen so you can't see the words you type, close your eyes, or write blindfolded. But don't edit! The muse wants a receptive mind, not an editor. If you edit while you write, you won't write. Be raw. Be courageous. Just *say* what you want to say. "Write it down first, later get it right" is a good slogan.

3. *Write a letter.* You probably find it easier to write a letter to a friend than an article for a magazine. Why? Because a letter is warm, personal, and focused. A lot of Hypnotic Writing shows up in personal letters. We become self-conscious when we write for the public. The trick is to write *everything* as a personal letter. Begin it with "Dear Mom," say your piece, and end it with "Love and hugs." Later on, edit out the mush. Ta-dah! There's your article!

4. *Use a prompt.* This is a major secret to creating Hypnotic Writing. Create a list of prompt words that you can draw on. Use these words to lead you into your next sentence. Examples of prompts are *because*, *and*, and *or*. Whenever you write and feel stuck for the next thought, take on a prompt word. The word will nudge you, or prompt you, into your next thought. For example, say you are writing the following line: "Hypnotic Writing caused the reader to stay glued . . ." and you can't think of what else to say. Just add a prompt word to your sentence and write down whatever comes to your mind. Example: "Hypnotic Writing causes the reader to stay glued *because* the sentences are so artfully done no one can resist them." Get the idea? The prompt word prompts you into another thought. Try it!

5. *Relax.* Put your pen down. Stretch. Close your eyes and take a deep, long breath. Let it out with a big *sigh*. Ahhhhhhhhh.

Feels good, doesn't it? The muse likes to visit relaxed writers, not uptight ones. As Charlie Parker said, "Don't play the saxophone. Let it play you."

Don't write. Let the writing write.
Think about it.

24

HOW TO NAIL YOUR READER'S ATTENTION

This may be the *MOST IMPORTANT CHAPTER* in this entire book.

Now ask yourself *why* I have your attention. What grabbed you? What made you want to keep reading? How come you're reading even now?

Let me take a guess:

First, I hit you—*hard*—with a simple but solid statement.
Second, I made the line stand out by presenting it on the page all by itself.
Third, I gave the line greater impact by capitalizing *some* of the words.

That's almost a formula for creating Hypnotic Writing. Almost but not quite. Hypnotic Writing requires relentless fine-tuning. Fidget with words and phrases and sentences until each line *kills*. Every line has to work to keep the reader sucked in and reading on.

How do you create writing of this caliber? Follow the basic Joe Vitale formula, which is *Write First, Edit Last*. First, get a rough draft down. Then, go back to edit it to perfection. A friend of mine, a sculptor, does something similar when he first sketches out his idea, then works to bring it into living form. And as E.B. White said, "There is no great writing, only great rewriting."

You create Hypnotic Writing in the rewriting stage. You take what you have and you whittle it—sculpt it—polish it—to perfection. Let me try to show you what I do with a few specific examples:

"The door was opened by Joe."

Say that's a line in an article you're working on. It's not bad, but it isn't good either. It's too passive. A minor tinkering can help this line out.

"Joe opened the door."

Getting better, isn't it? Now we have someone doing something. That's active and *much* more involving. There's life in the sentence now. But is it hypnotic? Nope. So let's try again:

"Joe kicked open the door."

That would grab your attention, wouldn't it? But I think we can do better.

"Joe *kicked* open the door!"

Now we have an irresistible line! Start your story with that one and your reader is bound to go on to the next one.

Every line has to work to keep your reader's attention. The radio is calling, the television is calling, the phone is ringing, the sun is shining, the refrigerator has food in it, there's a new movie at the theater—your lines have to keep your reader *nailed* to the page, or you'll lose them to any or all of the above. There are simply too many distractions in the world for you to offer mediocre writing. You don't have a choice. You *must* rewrite your material to perfection. You *must*!

Take my Thoughtline sales letter. Because my money was riding on the success of that letter, I *needed* it to work. If you come to your writing with the same attitude, that you *must* win, that your whole career is riding on this, then you will *make* it work.

I wanted Thoughtline to be a hit. But not a small hit. I wanted a *big, amazing, unforgettable, incredible, made me laugh all the way to the bank* hit.

I got it, too. But I had to rewrite the sales letter a hundred times. Let me give you a taste of what I did.

At one point in the original letter I said the following: "I was impressed when I used Thoughtline the first time."

Garbage! *Who cares*? So I rewrote the line to make it knock people off their chairs: "The first time I used Thoughtline it developed an outline for me that made my eyes pop!"

Notice the difference? I watched people as they read this new line and when they came across the words *eyes pop*, *their* eyes would widen—almost as if they were popping open. Amazing. Clearly a hypnotic line.

Here's another example: A client of mine is working on a new book. She was having trouble developing copy for the back cover, so she called me for some advice.

I told her, "Make every line *active* and *personal* and *alive!*"

She didn't understand. We set up a meeting for a consultation so I could walk her through the process.

"What do you want to say about your book?" I asked.

"I'll educate people about networking."

"How?" I inquired.

"By teaching them to use themselves resourcefully."

"Give me a specific tip."

"We say you are only four or five people away from anyone in the world," she explained. "If you use your network, you can meet anyone."

"Great! We'll use that for starters!" I said. And on a sheet of paper, I wrote the following: "You can reach anyone in the world through networking."

Then I looked at my client and told her what I was going to do.

"That line is bland," I told her. "Let's change it into a question and see if it's more intriguing."

I wrote the following: "Did you know you are only four or five people away from *anyone* in the world?"

Better, I thought to myself, but no cigar. I wrote another line down under it.

"Who do you need to see to get what you want?"

Still not good enough. My client observed it all with mounting excitement.

"Did you know you are only four or five people away from presidents, celebrities, millionaires, and royalty?"

Not bad!

"That's good!" my client said, smiling.

"It is," I admitted, "but we can do better. If you push past the obvious ideas, something deeper, and usually better, will come up."

"How do you make it better than that?" she asked.

"You can *always* make it better," I said. "One thing you can do is keep playing with the line until something triggers a breakthrough for you."

"That sounds like work to me."

"It is, it is," I agreed, "but it's an exhilarating challenge once you realize you are creating lines that actually influence people! They'll buy your ideas or products on the strength of what you write down. It's worth the extra work!"

I'm not sure if she bought my argument, but I still stand behind my words.

If you want to create writing that *nails* your readers to the page, *work at it*!

My client again looked at her new line. I stared at her for a moment, waiting for my unconscious to say something. I didn't have to wait long.

"You are only four people away from meeting *millionaires, celebrities*, or *greatness*! Who are those four people? Your *friends*!"

Getting better. We stopped there, but you can see how the process works. You keep trying ideas until something connects. Rewriting is the secret here. You rewrite and rewrite—always working to make your lines riveting—and you don't stop until you've succeeded.

In the next chapter I give you some specific ways to make your writing come *alive*!

25

HOW TO MAKE YOUR WRITING WALK, TALK, AND BREATHE

Now here are some ways to help you perfect, polish, and strengthen your writing. Apply these tools and you'll create writing that *walks, talks,* and *breathes*!

USE A THESAURUS

Obvious, isn't it? You've probably used a thesaurus at one time or another. Most writers use it for the wrong reasons, however. A still active myth is that writing has to be intellectual. Victims of this myth use a thesaurus to change simple words into complex ones.

Wrong! Use your thesaurus to make your writing simple and direct. If you have a long word, hunt down a shorter one. Mark Twain said he got paid the same amount whether he used the word *policeman* or *cop*. Since Twain was lazy, *cop* was easier to use—and quicker. Follow the same pattern. Find short words that say what you mean. Delete the long words. People trip over them.

Here's a rule of thumb: If you don't use the word in normal conversation, don't use it in your writing. Said another way: If you haven't heard the word at the airport or at a bus stop, don't use it.

Also use your thesaurus when you need a different word to say what you've already said. If you've been using the word *simple* several times in an article, find another word that says the same thing. Keep your writing fresh and your readers interested by finding simple words to express your thoughts.

Since I have an online thesaurus, I'll use it right now to find another word for *simple*.

As it turns out, there are a couple of dozen synonyms for *simple*. Even I was surprised! Here are a few words from the alternatives:

Clear	Natural
Intelligible	Neat
Lucid	Plain
Understandable	Unadorned
Unmistakable	Unaffected

Here's what I would do with this list: I'd scan it and look at all the *short* words that would fit in my writing. I'd skip words like *understandable*. Even though it is simple, I want the *most* direct word I can find. *Neat* and *plain* are good bets because they are only one syllable. *Lucid* sounds like it would work but I'm not sure everyone understands what it means. For that reason, I'd skip it.

A thesaurus is a handy tool to have at your side (or on your computer) because it gives you options. When you need a simple word to replace a long or complicated one, open your thesaurus. When you need to find a word to replace an overused one, use your thesaurus. It's a simple (there's that word again) but powerful way to make your writing hypnotic.

USE A SIMILE BOOK

As One Mad with Wine and Other Similes should also go on your shelf. I don't always find it inspiring, but using it is as compelling as a gun at your head. Thumb through it to find colorful phrases to clarify your writing.

A simile, by the way, is a phrase used to compare two different ideas. When I said the book was "as compelling as a gun at your head," I was using a simile.

A simile can give your reader a nice jolt. He's reading along and suddenly you make a comparison that surprises him. That's electrifying. If you say a man's smile was like a slit in the sidewalk, you used a simile and you gave your readers an image they can see.

When you use similes, you can make your own words

Fall softly as rose petals.
Gush out like toothpaste.
String and creep like insects!

Get the idea?

What about my client and the book on networking? How would she use similes to improve her writing?

There isn't a heading called Networking in the simile book I have, but there is one called Friendship. One simile we might use is "Life without a friend is like life without sun." Maybe my client would say, "Networking is as important to your life as sunshine."

Another simile in the book is "Without a friend the world is a wilderness." My client might say something like, "Without learning how to network, the world is a wilderness."

Using similes isn't always easy for me. Browsing through the collection and wondering how I can use these similes feels like swimming upstream in Jell-O. It's not at all like making instant coffee. (Notice the two similes?)

The effort is worth it, however. Every one of the paragraphs in this section was written with the help of my simile book. I feel my writing is better with similes. And probably clearer. Even though writing with similes sometimes feels like playing the piano with boxing gloves, I have to admit a good simile is like a loving kiss on a dark rainy day. It's nice.

Warning: Don't overuse similes. They are handy for putting some brightness in your writing, but if you overdo it, your readers will OD (overdose) and pass out. They will mentally fog over and no further thoughts will get through.

Spice up your articles and letters with a good simile and your writing will sell like cold lemonade at a marathon. Overdo it and your writing will read like an advertisement for jelly.

Got it?

USE A BOOK OF ANALOGIES

"Become a writing *wizard*! Turn your words into *spells* no mortal can resist!"

Those two lines were inspired by a brief glance into another book you need on your shelf: *The Analogy Book of Related Words* by Selma Glasser.

The book is billed as Your Secret Shortcut to Power Writing. I'm not sure if that's true, but the book can certainly tickle your mind into creating juicy new phrases. Glasser's book is a word-storming partner. Just open it to one of the several lists, all sorted by categories, and let your mind connect the words listed with the ideas you're trying to get across.

I was thinking of advertising this book when I opened her book to the category called Myth and Legend. I saw the word *wizard* and the word *spell* and I was suddenly inspired to write the line that began this section.

Here's a demonstration of how the book works:

Let's say I want to add spice to my client's book on networking. I open Glasser's book to *any* category. It falls open to Baseball and now I let my eyes roam the lists of related words. There's a *bag, ball, club, error, all-star, fastball* and a bunch more words.

And then it happens! Lightning strikes and—*aha!*—my mind makes a new connection!

"Don't strike out! Become a business all-star with these fastball concepts!"

See how it works?

Here's one more quick example: I'm thinking of how I can describe this book as I open Glasser's book to the category Chess. There's over a hundred words listed. Without more than a glance at the list I immediately have a new line:

"The strategies in this book will teach you how to checkmate the competition!"

I could go on and on. Use *The Analogy Book* to alter mediocre lines into sentences that tap dance and sing. You don't want to change every line into a new phrase, but doing it now and then adds incredible color to your writing.

Try it!

USE A BOOK OF QUOTES

> **Let us resolve to be masters, not the victims, of our history, controlling our own destiny without giving way to blind suspicions and emotions.**
>
> **—John F. Kennedy**

What does that quote have to do with Hypnotic Writing? Nothing. But it sure looks good on the page, doesn't it?

That's the first reason to use quotes: They are visually appealing. Readers want to see quotation marks in your writing. They want dialogue because dialogue is *alive*. Using quotes is one way to get dialogue (or what looks like dialogue) into your writing.

Considering all the books of quotations I see at the bookstores, I know that people love quotes. They are short, usually wise, often witty, and usually said by someone we all know (like Kennedy). The goal for you and me is to find quotes that *add* to our writing. Here's an example:

When I was working on my Thoughtline sales letter, I kept thumbing through books of quotations. One of my favorites is called *The Wit and Wisdom of Mark Twain*. As I was flipping through its pages, my eyes caught sight of this quote:

"A man's intellect is stored powder; it cannot touch itself off; the fire must come from the outside."

A light bulb flashed over my head (my wife saw it) and I knew that was the quote to include in my sales letter. So I used Twain's quote, added a line to make it even more relevant to my readers, and put it all into a box to make it stand out. The result was this:

Mark Twain wrote, "A man's intellect is stored powder; it cannot touch itself off; the fire must come from the outside." Thoughtline is the "fire" you need to make your mind *explode!*

Catches your eye, doesn't it?

Quotes add spice to your writing. Glance at any letter and if there's a quote, your eyes will spot it instantly. Quotes add aliveness, too, because they are perceived as *living*. Again, that's because people associate anything in quotations with dialogue, and dialogue is considered to be happening in real time (here and now). It's difficult to pass up anything with quotations in it.

Your quotes can't be very long, of course. Even quotation marks won't save you if your quote is several lines long. Again, you want to be short and sweet. Mark Twain's quote has a couple of breaks in it, but it is essentially only one line.

Your goal in selecting quotes is to find on that is

- Short (one line is best).
- Relevant (ties in with your point).
- Made by someone most of your readers will recognize (a celebrity or authority, like Twain or Kennedy).

Ivan Pavlov, the Russian scientist, said, "Men are apt to be much more influenced by words than by the actual facts of the surrounding reality."

Words have power. Words in a good quote can be powerful enough to alter the world. Whoever said the pen is mightier than the sword wasn't lying.

There are many good books of quotations available in the reference section of your favorite bookstore to help you in locating golden one-liners. Buy several and put them on the shelf along with your thesaurus and book of similes. They are all strong tools to help you create *irresistible writing.*

26

Give Me Some Meat!

Clarence Darrow was a famous trial lawyer. You have probably heard of him and his famous Monkey Trial. Or maybe you saw the one-man show where Henry Fonda portrayed the lawyer. Darrow was an idol of mine when I was a teenager. I almost became a lawyer due to his inspiring life. That great man once said:

"As long as the world shall last there will be wrongs, and if no man (or woman) objected and no man (or woman) rebelled, those wrongs would last forever."

I object to a practice far too many writers still believe in and use. I call these particular writers creators of "malnutritious writing." These are writers who leave out the vitamins in their writing—the facts. They feel that a knack for writing is all you need to persuade readers to listen to them.

These writers are "vegetarians" because their writing lacks meat. It lacks substance. It lacks credibility. They are so in love with their phrases that they overlook the need for reality.

There's an old joke about a writer who applies for a job at an advertising firm. The employer says, "Your resume consists of lies and empty statements. You got the job!"

The belief that too many writers still have is that a catchy letter or cute writing style is all you need. Sorry, Charlie. Readers are smarter than that. Frank Perdue of Perdue Farms stated that over 80 percent of all advertised products fail because the ads treat the consumers like fools.

People want *facts* and *benefits* and *solid ideas*. Joe Karbo wrote a book titled *The Lazy Man's Guide to Riches*. The book sold well and people still talk about Karbo's advertising. Karbo's long, wordy, personal ads were riveting. They motivated many people to buy his book.

But over 40% of his customers asked for a refund! Why?

Because Karbo didn't deliver. He created a powerful letter based on fluff. People fell for it. But nearly half asked for their money back. And nearly *all* of his customers never bought from him again.

Yet people still think Karbo (his name reminds me of karb-age) was a success. They are dazzled by the glittery writing and blind to the fact that the ad didn't get what it set out to get: results.

This happens even today. Major advertising firms are given awards even for their creative ads. Even when those ads didn't make a dent in sales. For example, people really love the Isuzu advertising. It's been rated as clever and creative. Yet the cars don't sell. Which means the ads don't work! So why are we applauding them?

A friend of mine told me my copywriting and letter-writing skills are so good he felt I ought to take some rocks out of my driveway and sell them as "lucky stones." He said people would buy them if I write strong enough copy to sell them.

That's a belief I am objecting to. Not only is it unethical to do what my friend suggested, I also think it is cruel. And from a realistic business stance, the idea is a dud. You may fool a reader once, but ultimately you'll lose him for life.

Robert Collier, the legendary copywriter who wrote *The Robert Collier Letter Book*, blew it once, too. He wrote up a powerful sales letter to market a series of books he hadn't even written yet. He wanted to test the product before he created it.

Collier made history. His letter brought in nearly a 100% response. People wanted his books! Collier had to write night and day in order to write those books and fulfill all the orders.

But almost half of his customers demanded refunds! Why?

Again, he had left out the meat. The facts. Collier promised more than he could deliver. In defense of Collier I admit that his books (which became *The Secret of the Ages*, a metaphysical classic now in its fiftieth printing) may have been ahead of their time. His customers may not have been ready for his ideas. Still, Collier didn't give the people the truth. He led them on.

Benjamin Franklin said the noblest question in the world is, "What good may I do in it?"

Are writers who offer empty phrases and flowery prose and advertise books not yet written doing well?

People aren't dumb. Burn them once and you lose them forever. Not only that, but research proves that those people will tell 8 to 10 other people about your crime. Furthermore, when any writer misleads a reader, he makes *all* writers look bad.

We all lose!

The techniques you're learning in this book will help you write material that will hold your reader's attention. But if you want to create Hypnotic Writing, you *must* work with real *facts* and real *benefits* and *solid ideas*.

Step two in my Turbocharge Your Writing formula encourages you to gather facts through research. Why? Because facts give your writing backbone. It gives your writing a spine. Without a spine, your writing will have all the impact of jelly.

Use facts. Give your writing some meat. Deal with the real world. Don't use words as sleight-of-hand devices to mislead your readers. Be honest.

Clarence Darrow was an honest lawyer who moved extremely opinionated people, even angry people, to see things his way. Darrow was a gifted speaker. He could hold a courtroom spellbound for *hours*. But his use of words depended on one essential ingredient, without which his life would have amounted to nothing: truth.

Think about it.

27

A WRITING
LESSON FROM THE
WORLD'S GREATEST
HYPNOTIST

P ull up a chair and sit down. Relax. Let me tell you a brief story
about the world's greatest hypnotist and how he learned an
important secret about writing.

Milton Erickson was legendary. He was considered the foremost
practitioner of hypnosis and became famous for his unique induction methods. Supposedly Erickson could put you into a trance
with a story—or by even shaking your hand. His innovative approaches to curing people have led to numerous books by him and
about him. Erickson himself was one of the three people who inspired the creation of Neuro-Linguistic Programming (NLP), a
new field of communication and behavioral study.

Erickson was often asked to write papers about hypnosis and
medical treatment. One day he faced a particularly difficult paper
and wasn't sure how to write it. What this colorful psychiatrist did
was brilliant.

Erickson put himself into a hypnotic trance and asked his unconscious mind for guidance. When he came out of the trance, he looked down and on his lap was a group of comic books. He didn't know what to think of them. He also didn't have any time to think about them. Right then the doorbell rang and Erickson had to go to see a client.

But he didn't forget about the comic books.

What did the comic books mean?

What was his unconscious telling him?

What do *you* think was going on?

Erickson realized—maybe the next day—that comic books are written in a very simple and direct style. There are very few words, lots of pictures, and every idea gets communicated in a brief but effective way. Everyone understands comics.

That was it!

Erickson understood that his unconscious mind was urging him to write his paper in the same way comic books are written—simply, clearly, and directly. There's no need to use big words or confusing concepts. Just say what you have to say in terms even a child could understand.

Aha! That was another insight!

Comic books are written so children can make sense of them. They are also written so adults can appreciate them. Erickson knew he had to communicate his ideas so simply that even a child could grasp his meaning. He knew that if he expressed himself in simple terms, every adult would be able to understand him.

This is an important lesson for you and me.

What I encourage writers to do is pretend they are writing their letter or article for children. If you can imagine a child reading—and understanding—your writing, then you will write in a way that *everyone* will understand. In fact, go out and *find* a child and talk to him about your next writing project. That child will help you clarify what you are trying to say.

Communication, after all, is *your* responsibility. If someone doesn't understand your writing, it means you didn't succeed in writing clear and direct material.

Fyodor Dostoyevsky said, "If people around you will not hear you, fall down before them and beg their forgiveness, for in truth, you are to blame."

Erickson was a genius. And what he learned about writing applies to every writer. You may not be writing for children, and you may not be writing comic books, but you must always remind yourself that there is a child in every reader. Speak to that child, and you will succeed in communicating to your reader.

More than that, when you speak to the child in your reader, you speak directly to *his* unconscious mind. Few people can resist what their inner child likes. Speak to the child and you will hold his attention.

Erickson himself said in a 1966 lecture, ". . . the unconscious mind is decidedly simple, unaffected, straightforward and honest. . . . It is rather simple, rather childish."

Your assignment: Read a comic book!

28

ELECTRIFYING TIPS FOR CREATING BREAKTHROUGH WRITING

Are there any secrets to writing clear, crisp, alive—even break-through—material?

You bet!

But they have more to do with how you think as you write than with any before or after writing techniques. Here they are.

SEE THE EVENTS

As you write, visualize the material you are writing about. If you can see the characters, the action, the scene, the product, or whatever, then your reader will see it with you. There is a subtle link connecting your brain with your hand that enables you to innocently convey what you see to your readers. It happens automatically. As you write, visualize what you are writing about, and your words will naturally fit the image.

Another approach is to visualize your reader. If you know your reader, perfect. If you don't, try to conjure up an image of who you think your reader is. As you'll see in a second, writing to *a* person, an individual, is powerful.

WRITE TO ONE PERSON

You've heard this one before, but it's worth repeating. You can feel overwhelmed when you write something for "the public." Don't write for the masses. Write for one person. Write to an individual, any individual, and you will create a personal rapport with your readers. Though thousands of people may read your articles, they only read it individually. Write your material to one person, as if writing a letter, and you will naturally create a personal aura in your writing.

You've gotten personal letters from friends, and you've gotten form letters that had your name inserted into them. You could tell the difference, couldn't you? Form letters—even if they plug your name into the copy—are wooden. Hypnotic Writing requires personal contact. No matter what you are writing, write it to *one* person and you'll create a sense of friendliness that can't be beat.

GET EXCITED

As you write, *feel* what you are trying to convey. Let some emotions seep in. When you tell a story in person to someone you feel comfortable with, you move your hands, change voice inflections, raise and squint your eyes, and much more. You become animated and alive. But you may become aloof and dignified when you write about the same story. The result is a dud. Put *excitement* into your writing. Let go. Feel emotion. Get moved and you'll move your reader.

You can test this for yourself. Go to a party and watch the life of the party. He or she tells stories with great passion and verve. Take that same individual, put a pen into his or her hand, and say, "Write out the story you told at the party." They freeze! Most of us do. Instead, let go. Write your letters and articles with all the spontaneous energy and enthusiasm you have. Be yourself. Don't write to impress; write to share a feeling.

GET TO THE POINT

We're all busy. We're flooded with sensory input and the world demands our attention. Keeping focused on long words, long sentences, long paragraphs, or long books is almost impossible. Do *you* like run-on sentences or complicated phrases? Probably not. Keep this in mind as you write. Say what you have to say and cut out any needless words, sentences, and so on.

Write to a child—someone who will listen to you only as long as you are concise and interesting—and you'll write to all of us.

DON'T JUDGE

You have no idea whether what you want to write is great or something less. You can't be the judge of your own material. Your readers cast the deciding vote, not you. Do the best you can, polish your writing to the best of your ability, and let your readers decide. And while they are deciding, keep writing.

Judging your work slows you down. It will sometimes stop you dead in your tracks. Several times I have begun a piece of writing, judged it as lousy, and stopped. Weeks or months later I would stumble across the unfinished work and reread it. It looked good! It read well and was really going somewhere. Why hadn't I completed it? Now it was too late to iron it out because I had lost the initial momentum. Then I would kick myself all over the room for *not* finishing it!

Since you aren't buying your writing, let the people who are judge it. Don't listen to your Mr. Editor as you write. Your job is to write. Period.

Got it?

29

A CASE AGAINST PERFECTION

What? A case *against* perfection?

I am not encouraging you to be sloppy.

I am urging you to keep writing once you've begun and don't stop until you've hit the finish line for that draft.

And I'm urging you to edit your work following the steps I give you in a moment.

What I am saying here is that too many writers (including me) begin a project, judge it as pretty bad, and quit. They quit because their writing doesn't look "perfect."

And too many writers (including me) begin to edit their work and then either: (1) decide the project is trash and dump it into a file, or (2) decide the project needs a *lot* of rewriting and then spend weeks, months, even *years* on it!

No! Finish what you started—*fast*! Complete it, edit it, rewrite it, polish it—, and then get it *out the door*!

I have learned that this is a fundamental key to success: Don't wait for perfection.

John Ruskin said, "No good work whatever can be perfect, and the demand for perfection is always a sign of a misunderstanding of the ends of art."

Perfection is your enemy. Do the best you can and move on to the next project. Striving for perfection can stop you from achieving any results. Go for results.

The more you do, the better you get. Quantity leads to quality. Ray Bradbury wrote 2,000 stories in order to get 200 that were classics. Some authors write six books in order to have two that are worth publishing. Don't judge your work as you write it, just write it! Crank out the stuff!

Again, I am not urging you to crank out crap. I want you to write spellbinding, unforgettable, *Hypnotic Writing*.

But too many writers spend *too much* time fiddling with their work. In the next section I give you some eye-opening ways to edit your work. Follow my suggestions, rewrite your work, and then let it go. Don't dwell on it!

Look! Your writing *can't* be perfect. Not ever!

Here's why: If you're writing something for an editor, that editor is going to change your work. He or she will alter words, sentences, and passages; delete or add sections; change your title and more. You can spend all year beating your head against your computer screen, but no matter how much work you put into perfecting your writing, your editor is gonna change it. Trust me. As H.G. Wells said, "There's no passion equal to the passion to alter someone's draft."

The strange thing is, your readers will *never* know what your editor changed! I remember sending a review to a major magazine. I polished that thing till its perfection blinded me. But when the review came out, the last two paragraphs—two *entire* paragraphs—had been sliced off! I thought the review was a mess without those last lines but no one ever noticed the change—except me. The readers simply accepted the published review as is.

If you're writing something for the public, say a sales letter or a newsletter, you are going to have some people say your writing isn't clear. When I wrote a sales letter on myself as a ghostwriter, some people wrote back with suggestions on how I could perfect it. One person went through my letter and highlighted—in bright yellow—every time I used the words *I* or *my*. He suggested "I" delete those words! And when I wrote a newsletter for a client of mine, some readers said it was too folksy and some said it wasn't folksy enough.

Remember my sales letter on Thoughtline? I rewrote that thing a hundred times—maybe more—yet it still isn't considered perfect. Just the other day I received an anonymous note from someone in response to that sales letter. She (or he) said, "I think this is a horrible package you are offering, as it will contribute to the already illiterate, lazy-minded folks in this country. Please put your intelligence and energy into a better serving area!"

What's "perfect writing" then?

I have no idea. What's perfect to me may seem like a baby's first draft to my agent. My job as a writer is to do the best I can. That means writing with skill and precision, and then editing ruthlessly. It also means letting go of the writing so it can go out into the world and get whatever results it's going to get.

You'll learn more from the feedback you get than from the rewriting you do. Input will give you concrete direction; rewriting will give you hand cramps.

Again, I am *not* saying mediocre writing is okay (though it often gets published).

My message is this: Don't let striving for perfection stand in the way of getting results.

Finish the drafts you start. Edit the best you can. Then let your work go.

30

HOW TO PERSUADE READERS TO YOUR SIDE

Sooner or later you will have to write a letter or document to sell someone something. How will you do it? How will you persuade people to your way of thinking? This is probably the most challenging assignment there is when it comes to creating Hypnotic Writing.

I find the whole subject of persuasion absolutely riveting. I am fascinated by what it takes to move people, to motivate them, to get them to act. As you and I both know, the pen is powerful. Writing can cause—or stop—wars. Writing can make—or break—sales campaigns.

What does it take to create Hypnotic Writing that persuades people to *your* way of thinking? That's the subject of this section. Here are the steps I think you need to keep in mind when attempting to create writing that sways people.

KNOW WHAT YOU WANT

Before you do anything you must know what *you* want to accomplish. What is your goal? What is your objective? When people read your letter (or advertisement or whatever it might be), what do you want them to do?

This is step one in *Turbocharge Your Writing.* Everything you write will fall into line to support your objective once you *state* your objective. The great baseball player Babe Ruth was known for walking up to the plate and pointing to where he intended to hit the ball. Ruth was a showman and his pointing thrilled people, but it also helped him hit more home runs than anyone else in history at that time. Babe Ruth stated his intention ("I'm going to hit the ball there") and, more often than not, he did exactly what he said he would.

What action do you want your readers to take? Shoot for the moon. When I created a letter to send to managers about my writing seminars, I wanted a 100% response. I wanted *every* manager to read the letter, get excited, and call me.

That didn't happen. But my grand objective helped me write one of the most powerful and persuasive letters in my own literary history.

What do *you* want your letter to accomplish?

EMOTIONAL APPEAL

Back in the sixties Roy Garn wrote an eye-opening book called *The Magic Power of Emotional Appeal.* I doubt if it's still in print, but hunt down a copy. You'll learn a lot about how to write—or speak—in a way that captures people and makes them listen.

Garn's premise is that everyone—including you and me—is preoccupied. You have stuff on your mind. You're worried about money, work, your children, a new relationship, and the future. Or maybe you're thinking about sex, or a new movie you want to see, or a health problem. There's something on your mind right now, even as you read these words, that tugs at your attention. Right?

Our challenge as writers and speakers is to break people out of their preoccupation so they can hear what we have to say. If you don't shake your readers, they'll stay preoccupied and your writing will go into one ear and out the other—if it gets into an ear at all.

How do you break your reader's preoccupation?

A joke, a quote, a story, a statistic, a headline, a name—all of these can help awaken people so they will take in your message. But the hook has to be relevant. For example, I used a headline on my Thoughtline sales letter that spoke to the interests of the people getting it. Another tactic I could have used was to begin with a quote from a major league author (say Ray Bradbury or Stephen King) who uses the software. That would have gotten attention, too.

Another approach is to meet your readers right where they are preoccupied. For example, if you are contacting writers, one concern (or preoccupation) of writers is the need to be published. So speak to that need. Tell those writers you can help them get published, and you'll connect with their emotional preoccupation.

You have to ask yourself, "What does my reader care about?" and "What is on my reader's mind?" The people you are writing to probably have a common concern, problem, or complaint. Your letter should address that issue in a way that captures their attention.

Give this topic some deep thought. Emotions move people. Appeal to your reader's main concerns and you'll tap into their emotions with genuine appeal. And when you successfully do that, your writing becomes hypnotic!

GIVE THEM WHAT THEY WANT

What do your readers want? No doubt they want real solutions to real problems. They don't want features, they want benefits. What's the difference? A feature is saying the new car is blue; a benefit is saying the new car is blue because studies show blue cars are in less accidents and therefore are much safer. A feature states a fact. A benefit states why the fact is important to your reader.

Your readers want what all of us want: happiness, an easier life, security, entertainment. Can you give it to them?

ASK QUESTIONS THAT LEAD TO YOUR SIDE

"If there were a way for you to write easily and powerfully, would you want it?"

Notice there's only one way to answer the question. Unless your reader is not interested in writing (again, you should be offering people what they want), then your readers have to answer the question with a *yes!*

Another example: "If I could get you a new car at a monthly price you can afford, and with all the options you want, would you be interested in seeing it?"

Assuming the person being asked is shopping for a car, what do you think they will say?

Another example: "If I could give you a marketing strategy that is guaranteed to increase your profits, would you be interested?"

Of course!

USE WORD PICTURES

Studies prove that we think in pictures. Describe your views, or your product, in vivid detail. Tell people what they will see, feel, hear, and taste when they use your new blender (or whatever). Paint a living portrait that people can see as they read your words.

One secret to doing this is to tell your reader exactly what happens when they use your product.

"When you turn on your computer, Thoughtline comes up, greets you by name, and then begins to ask questions about your project. You type in your answers and then Thoughtline asks you another question based on what you entered. Imagine how it feels to talk to your computer—and it actually talks back!"

Get the picture?

USE TESTIMONIALS

Do you know what people don't have anymore? Trust. The number one reason mail order campaigns fail and sales letters live in the dumpster is because your readers don't trust you. People have been ripped off so many times that they are *extremely* hesitant to gamble on a new thing.

Get testimonials from people who have used your product. If the quotes are from people we all know—such as celebrities—all the better. They give your writing credibility.

One tip: Be sure the testimonials are specific. "I liked the book" isn't as strong as "The chapter on negotiation helped me land a contract for $39,000!"

How do you get testimonials? Ask for them from people who have used your product. If they don't want to write one, write it for them and have them sign it.

Another way to be sure to gain your readers' trust is to offer a solid guarantee. Fact is, without a guarantee, few—if anyone—will order what you are selling or believe what you are saying.

REMIND THEM OF THE PROBLEM AND YOUR SOLUTION

Before you end your letter, remind your readers that they have a problem. Use that emotional appeal I mentioned earlier. Say, "If you're tired of receiving rejection slips, order my book today and put an end to your frustration."

Murray Raphel, co-author of *The Great Brain Robbery* and *The Do-It-Yourself Mail-Order Handbook* says fear is a great motivator. I don't encourage you to frighten people into seeing things your way, but I *do* suggest you gently remind your readers that they have a problem and you have a solution.

ADD A P.S.

Think about it. When you receive a letter—any letter—what do you read first? The P.S. We all do it. Studies show that the postscript is *the* most often read and first read part of any letter.

Your P.S. is your chance to state your strongest point, or to offer your guarantee, or to mention just how wonderful your product is. You might want to put your heaviest ammunition into your P.S. because it's the section people will read first *and* last—and the one they'll remember longest.

BE VISUALLY ATTRACTIVE

This means use short paragraphs, dialogue when appropriate, bullets, and wide margins (a staggered right margin aids readability, by the way).

If you pick up a letter and it is a solid block of type, do you want to read it? Probably not. It's not inviting. It looks like work.

Instead, make your writing attractive. How you lay out your letter can make people like it before they even read it. I suggest you play around with how your letter looks so it gives a very interesting first impression.

BE SOLD ON WHAT YOU'RE SELLING

This may be the most important point. You can't sell what you don't believe in. This is a fundamental law in persuasion. How can you sell a car you wouldn't drive yourself or a book you haven't read or a software program you don't use? *You can't!*

Enthusiasm sells people. And you cannot persuade anyone of anything unless you are first convinced. Emotional appeal and all the other tips will fall in line if *you* are sold on what you are saying. Don't try to write anything if you don't honestly believe in what you are writing about.

Follow these guidelines, think about your readers' emotional concerns, and talk to them in a way they can't ignore. If you do so, you'll create writing that is both persuasive *and* hypnotic.

31

WARP SPEED EDITING SECRETS WORTH KILLING FOR

Is editing important? Listen to Ernest Hemingway: "Most writers slough off the most important part of their trade—editing their stuff, honing it and honing it until it gets an edge like a bullfighter's killing sword."

Here's the way I look at it: Editing and rewriting, the last stage in my *Turbocharge Your Writing* formula, is your opportunity to be sure you hit the target you were aiming for. In step one you said you wanted to create something specific. The next step (rewriting) is your chance to see if you did it.

This step is where you invite Mr. Editor, that voice of criticism in your head, back. Why? Because now you want all the help you can get. You want your writing to be as perfect as you can get it.

I've found most people don't know *how* to edit their work. They write their drafts, check the spelling (sometimes) and punctuation (even less often), and send the work out. Sadly, these writers are sending out trash.

How do you edit your work? In this section I offer you some

powerful ways to hone your writing so it has the razor's edge Hemingway wanted.

Here goes.

CUT OFF THEIR HEADS

Look at your writing and examine the first few paragraphs. Can you delete them? Will the article still stand if you dump the first and second paragraphs?

If you're writing a book, look at the first chapter. Can you drop it? Can the book stand without it?

Bruce Barton, author of the 1925 bestseller *The Man Nobody Knows*, once said writers start writing something before they start saying something.

In a short article, those first few paragraphs are suspect. Consider deleting them. In a longer work, like a book, that first chapter can probably be deleted. Why? As Barton suggested, those early . lines are "warm-ups." You probably don't really need them.

As a book reviewer I used to see a lot of self-published books. These writers almost always could have deleted their first chapters. They were just too much in love with their own words to cut them out.

As a magazine journalist, I have worked hard to create opening paragraphs that were "grabbers." Yet all too often the editors deleted my lead. Nobody ever complained!

Look at your opening paragraphs. Can you drop them? I am not saying you must slice them out. I am suggesting you examine that area, as it is a place where you can trim your writing.

CUT OFF THEIR FEET

By the same token, look at the endings of your writings.

In an article, look at the last couple of paragraphs. Do you really need them?

In a book, look at the last chapter. Can you throw it out and still have a solid book?

Probably. Again, this area is often weak. Don't automatically delete your endings, but *do* look at them with a critical eye.

CUT OUT EVERY SIXTH WORD

An editor in California, DeWitt Scott once co-created a computer program that automatically knocked out every sixth word in his writings. Scott realized that though the program often deleted words that he needed, it also showed him that he could edit his writing more ruthlessly.

Look at your own stuff. What if you deleted every sixth word— or every third word—or even every fourth sentence?

No doubt you would sometimes lose a word or phrase you needed. But I bet you'd learn that you could tighten your writing, too. Readers today want concise, simple writing. Delete everything that doesn't serve your writing. Trim the fat. If that means knocking out every sixth word, then do it!

Sometimes writers tell me they can't possibly tighten their writing. It's perfect as it is, they say.

"Could you trim your writing if you were offered $1,000 to do so?" I ask. They sure can! Your writing isn't carved in stone. It's plastic. You can change it, delete it, and redo it.

Remember the "delete every sixth word" program as you reread your writing. It will help you strengthen your material. Also remember the great quote from novelist Elmore Leonard: "I try to leave out the parts people skip."

TAKE STEPHEN KING'S ADVICE

Best-selling horror novelist Stephen King suggests you make 10 copies of your work and hand them to 10 friends. Invite their feedback. Ask them to edit your writing. Tell them to feel free to say whatever they want.

Yes, you are opening yourself to heavy gunfire. But you will also get a lot of editorial feedback—*free*!

The trick is to not take anything personally. Pretend you're a researcher. All you're doing is taking a poll. Who likes your writing? Who doesn't? What do they like? What do they hate?

King suggests that you look for the similarities in the feedback you get. In other words, if most of your 10 readers say they can't understand Chapter 5 in your book, then check out that chapter. But if you get a few isolated comments, don't worry about them. You can't please everyone.

Again, what you are looking for is the majority opinion. If all 10 people hate your title, *change your title*! But if only one person complains, I wouldn't bother about it.

GET SOMEONE TO READ IT OUT LOUD TO YOU

To me, this is *the* most powerful and illuminating way to find out where your writing stands.

Hand your writing to a friend and ask them to read it *aloud* to you. Why? Because this makes the reading process visible. When your friend reads the material, listen to them and watch them. If they have to reread lines, or stumble over some words, or wrinkle their brow, then those are areas that need to be rewritten!

When you send your writing to an agent or editor or customer, you have no idea what they will find difficult to read. They read your words in their office, and you can't tell what they think. But when you have someone to read the material out loud, right in front of you, the entire process becomes obvious. Any troublesome, hard to read areas will be blazingly apparent.

Hypnotic Writing has to be easy, simple, and clear to be effective. When someone reads your material to you, you will easily spot where you need to correct your prose.

READ IT OUT LOUD

This is a poor second choice to the earlier step. But reading your work to yourself *will* give you a different perspective. For that reason, it's worth doing. The trouble with this step is that you wrote the piece, so you know how the words are to be read. Any problem areas will be less obvious to you.

GET *FREE* HELP

I don't dwell on grammar in my classes for the simple reason that if you follow my *Turbocharge Your Writing* formula, your grammar will *automatically* improve. Studies have shown that when you let go of your obsession with editing, you'll naturally write material that adheres to the rules of grammar.

Still, support is available.

First, I suggest you use a computer grammar checker.

Second, you can always call for help. There are grammar hotlines around the country.

TAKE A BREAK

Put your writing away for three days to three weeks. Get some distance between you and your work. Why? Because you'll see your writing with clear eyes after you've looked elsewhere for a while.

This doesn't mean you get to take a vacation after every draft you write. Instead, begin a NEW writing project. Just quit working on this one for a while.

Have you ever gotten to see a letter you wrote a few months after you had sent it? I have. And I've been amazed at the typos and ambiguous sentences I've seen. When I read the letter right after writing it, I "saw" what I knew was supposed to be there. But later on, days or weeks or months down the road, when I had the chance to see the letter again, all my errors were *obvious*.

Take a break—even 15 minutes—and then return to editing your work.

CUT AND PASTE

Before I had a computer I would type out my drafts, cut out each paragraph, and then shuffle them into new piles. Each stack was related by theme or idea or character. Then I'd retype the article from the new arrangement. It worked every time.

Your first draft isn't written in stone. You can change the order, delete entire sections, write entire new ones, cut and paste to your heart's content. No one will be the wiser.

REMEMBER KISSINGER

In *Turbocharge Your Writing,* I tell a story about politician Henry Kissinger that is worth repeating here:

> Kissinger assigned a writing project to one of his aides. The aide wrote the piece and sent it in. But the next day the manuscript was back on the aide's desk with a yellow note from Kissinger saying, "You can do better."
>
> The aide reworked the material and again sent it in. Next day the aide found the same manuscript back on his desk with yet another note that said, "You can do better."
>
> The aide rewrote the material, ruthlessly edited it, added some powerful facts and figures, proofread it, and then hand-delivered it. He told Kissinger, "Sir, this is the best I can do."
>
> Kissinger accepted the manuscript and said, "In that case, I'll read it."

Kissinger had never read those earlier drafts! He had simply tricked the aide into doing the best work possible.

You can always do better. Now, whenever I finish a project, I ask myself, "Can you do better?"

If I'm honest with myself, I know I can.

ONE LAST WORD

When do you stop rewriting?

How do you know when your work is polished?

I don't know. I'm not sure anyone does.

My rule of thumb is to do the very best work I can, to see if I have met my objective (if I have done what I set out to do), and then to let the writing go. You can spend years rewriting your material. Don't! Do your best and send the work out. The feedback you get will help you do any more rewriting.

Consider what Albert Einstein said: "Everything should be made as simple as possible, but not simpler."

32

HOW TO MAKE YOUR WRITING SEXY

Sex is hypnotic. That's why it is used so blatantly in advertisements. How do you give your writing sex appeal?

It's easier than you think. I'll give you a clue. Which do you like to read: a novel by William Faulkner or your favorite mail order catalog?

The key to creating sexy writing is *format*.

William Faulkner was a literary genius who created classic novels. But his writing often had pages (pages!) of *solid type*. Talk about run-on sentences! You might have to search an entire chapter to find *one* period. Yes, Faulkner is considered a legend. No, most readers today don't want to see a solid block of type. It's not very attractive.

FOUR WAYS TO MAKE YOUR WRITING MORE INVITING

To avoid a solid block of type:

1. Use bullets.
2. Use quotes.
3. Use itsy-bitsy paragraphs.
4. Use boxes.

Here's a quick explanation of each.

Bullets

A bullet is a dot or star or asterisk. (See Chapter 10.) You can use bullets anywhere, anytime, and they will always work. They are a way to list ideas or key points. Readers love 'em!

Quotes

Readers love quotes. Put something in quotation marks and it'll be read before anything else. Why? Because people are interested in people. They want to know what was said, not what you want to say. As Horace said, "The musician who always plays on the same string is laughed at." (Think about it.)

Little Paragraphs

Break up your paragraphs into one or two lines each. Stagger their length so they don't become predictable. Which would you read first: a letter single-spaced with a two-line first paragraph, a three-line second one, a one-line third one, and so on?

Take a look at the following letters and tell me which is easier to read (they are the same letter):

Example One

How many times have you read a memo and then called the author of it to find out what was meant? How often do the reports you see need to be explained in a follow-up meeting? Poor written communication costs you and your business time and money. You know it. I know it. But what can you do about it? Give me two hours—even one hour—and I can teach you and your associates how to *Turbocharge Your Writing!* I'm a professional writer and the author of three books on writing. Over the years I have developed a new way to perfect writing. My seven-step breakthrough formula has already helped hundreds of people vastly improve their writing. They now write memos, letters, and reports that are easy, clear, and direct. Ask the people I have already taught—everyone from writers, editors, speakers, psychologists, engineers, salespeople, lawyers, computer programmers, and high school students to clerks, accountants, and executives. Everyone is *satisfied!* My program is exciting, unique, and innovative. What I offer you is a tested strategy—a proven technique—that gets results. And it's guaranteed to work. I'm so sure you will profit from my *Turbocharge Your Writing* program that I will guarantee it—unconditionally. I'll come in, do the program for your group, and let you decide just how truly beneficial it is. Call me for details. Call within three days and I'll send you a free copy of my best-selling booklet, *Turbocharge Your Writing!* You have nothing to lose—and a lot of time and money to save!

Example Two

How many times have you read a memo and then called the author of it to find out what was meant? How often do the reports you see need to be explained in a follow-up meeting?

Poor written communication costs you and your business time and money. You know it. I know it. But what can you do about it?

Give me two hours—even one hour—and I can teach you and your associates how to *Turbocharge Your Writing!*

I'm a professional writer and the author of three books on writing. Over the years I have developed a new way to perfect writing.

My seven-step breakthrough formula has already helped hundreds of people vastly improve their writing. They now write memos, letters, and reports that are easy, clear, and direct.

Ask the people I have already taught—everyone from writers, editors, speakers, psychologists, engineers, salespeople, lawyers, computer programmers, and high school students to clerks, accountants, and executives. *Everyone is satisfied!*

My program is exciting, unique, and innovative. What I offer you is a tested strategy—a *proven* technique—that gets results.

And it's guaranteed to work. I'm so sure you will profit from my *Turbocharge Your Writing* program that I will guarantee it—unconditionally. I'll come in, do the program for your group, and let you decide just how truly beneficial it is.

Call me for details. Call within three days and I'll send you a free copy of my best-selling booklet, *Turbocharge Your Writing!*

You have nothing to lose—and a lot of time and money to save!

Pretty obvious which letter has sex appeal, isn't it?

BOXES

People read whatever you put into a box.

Yes, you can make your writing "sexy." Those tips will work every time. Try it and see.

33

How People Think

As I mentioned earlier, the average web site (or sales letter) is terrible. They are written by people talking about themselves and begging you to buy from them. In order for you to be different, you'll need to write in the way people think. You'll need to create Hypnotic Writing in my favorite of all forms: the story.

Once upon a time Roger Schank, writing in his thought-provoking scholarly book *Tell Me a Story*, stated, "We do not easily remember what other people have said if they do not tell it in the form of a story. We can learn from the stories of others, but only if what we hear relates strongly to something we already knew." Elsewhere he writes, "People think in terms of stories."

In short, if you want to create Hypnotic Writing that follows the basic three-step formula I've taught you, then the best form may be through a story.

I love stories. My most successful articles, books, web sites, and even audiopackages, all include stories. Stories are a powerful way to get your message across. People don't usually defend against a story. And, as Schank pointed out, people actually *think* in stories.

If you remember one definition we gave earlier—"Anything you do that makes your listeners react because of *mental images* you plant in their minds is *waking hypnosis*"—then you can easily see that written stories are a terrific way to create mental images that lead to a waking trance.

When people read your story, it takes place in their head. This is a powerful place for you to be. You are in a person's operating control panel. The more you cause them to think in terms of mental images, the closer you will get to causing them to take action at your web site. In short, stories are a potent tool.

But how do you create a story composed of Hypnotic Writing that actually moves people to action?

Let's look at that next.

34

HOW TO CREATE HYPNOTIC STORIES

This is easier than you might think. What you want to do is remember a true story that happened as a result of someone using your product or service. It needs to be true because I'm trying to spread honesty and good will across the Internet and everywhere else. It also needs to be true so the FTC doesn't jump on you for fabrications in your promise. Finally, if it's true, it's easier to write.

For example, I recently recorded Dr. Robert Anthony's powerful material *Beyond Positive Thinking*, which I think is the holy grail of self-improvement wisdom. When I was creating the web site to promote the CD set—which you can see over at http://www.Beyond PositiveThinking.com—I asked Dr. Anthony to give me a few stories of how people used his famous material to get results in their lives. One of the stories he gave me is now on the site. Here it is.

The Story of Ramon
Dr. Robert Anthony
Many years ago I met a man named Ramon. In fact, I dedicated an entire chapter to him in my book *Doing What You Love—Loving What You Do*. Ramon is one of the most successful businessmen in California as well as one of the most spiritually evolved beings I have ever met.

I met Ramon because a friend had given him a copy of Beyond Positive Thinking. Ramon buys every self-improvement tape album sold. He has all of Nightingale-Conant's products, plus more. He never plays the radio in his Rolls Royce. Instead, he listens to personal development programs on his 60-minute ride to and from his office—even though he is already a successful multimillionaire.

Ramon told me, "Your Beyond Positive Thinking recordings are the best ever produced by anyone. I should know, I own all of them!"

He was so impressed at how they could help other people, he would buy 25 sets at a time and put them into the trunk of his Rolls Royce. Anytime he met someone whom he felt needed help, he would give them a set free of charge. He frequently called me to tell me of the "miraculous" results they had had with the tapes and how it had changed their lives.

Over the years he has bought over 300 sets from me and to this day says that he has never found anything more powerful to change lives than Beyond Positive Thinking.

As you can see, that story silently communicates an almost hypnotic message: *Dr. Robert Anthony's recordings work.*

Had I just come out and said, "Dr. Robert Anthony's methods work," you could dismiss the thought. You might think I am just trying to sell you something. But when someone else proves the statement without actually saying it, through a captivating story, then the message goes right into people's unconscious mind. You slipped in past their mental radar.

Of course, someplace on your web site you might declare: "Dr. Robert Anthony's methods work." That's fine. Declarations can be hypnotic, too. That's why hypnotists say "You are getting sleepier and sleepier" and not "Are you getting sleepy yet?"

Commands work. But what I am advising you to do here is to *also* create a story that conveys the same message. This way you are speaking to people's conscious as well as subconscious minds.

I learned about the power of stories from Jack London, Mark Twain, Robert Collier, Shirley Jackson, and from the greatest hypnotist of all time: Milton Erickson.

Erickson was an eccentric, highly skilled therapist. He used the patient's problem to solve their problem. If someone walked in complaining of a nervous tick, Erickson might use that tick in some hypnotic way. He might ask the person to see if they could speed it up, or slow it down. Erickson, in short, helped people regain control.

What I just told you is a hypnotic story. It is entertaining, educational, and even hypnotic. It conveys several messages. Some you got consciously. Some you got unconsciously.

Do you see the power in a story?

Let me share with you one of my popular articles on the magic power of a good story.

How One Hypnotic Story Brought
15 Automatons to My Door
Joe Vitale

In 1844 the great circus promoter P.T. Barnum bought an automaton from the famous magician, Eugene Robert-Houdin.

An automaton is a mechanical device that imitates life. Think of them as early robots. In the middle of the eighteenth century, automatons were all the rage: mechanical ducks and elephants, pictures with moving parts, even human androids that could write, draw, and play musical instruments. They were haunting, magical, intricate, detailed, and usually meticulously crafted out of watch parts, metal, and wood.

The one Robert-Houdin created was a life-sized figure able to write and draw, and even answer simple questions. He once displayed it before the king of France. Barnum heard of it on his tour in Europe with General Tom Thumb and bought it. But that legendary automaton was lost in one of Barnum's many fires.

I spoke to a few people who still build automatons—which is an almost lost art today—to see if someone could rebuild the one Robert-Houdin made and Barnum owned. Most said it would cost about a quarter of a million dollars and take well over a year to complete.

I passed.

But then one day a month or so ago I got a call from a potential new client. He was a delight to talk to. He performs magic, runs a speakers bureau, and was familiar with most of my books. During the course of our lively conversation he floored me by announcing that he inherited a few automatons.

I couldn't believe it.

"You what!" I blurted, almost too excited to speak.

"I have some automatons my best friend made," he explained. "He left them to me in his will."

"How many do you have?"

"Oh, I dunno, maybe fifteen."

"Fifteen?!?" I mumbled, truly shaken to the core that he had any automatons let alone over a dozen of them.

"I have one that does mind reading and another that levitates," he said. "They all do something different."

You can't imagine how stunned I was to hear about this. It was like finding the Holy Grail of Automatons. While these particular devices are all modern and nowhere near as valuable as the one made by the great magician Robert-Houdin, any automaton today is a rare and collectible item.

I was intrigued.

And I wanted those automatons.

"How much do you want for them?" I asked.

"I could never sell them," he said. "I inherited these from a man who lived to be ninety and treated me like his own son. I've got them in storage."

At that point I did something naturally and instantaneously. Right there on the spot I weaved a hypnotic story that changed my life—and his.

Here's how it went.

"I understand how you feel," I began. "About twenty years ago, the landlord I had at the time knew I was into music. He heard me play the harmonica and knew I had an interest in learning to play the guitar. One day, he just gave me a guitar he had for over fifty years. He just handed it to me. But he said one thing I never forgot: 'You can give it away but you can never sell it.' I promised him I would keep my word. I still have that guitar today. I'm never going to sell it but I will give it away when the right person comes along."

Well, that hypnotic story did the trick. The prospect on the phone heard my story and in his mind he heard the phrase, "It's okay to give the automatons to Joe but you can't sell them to him."

All we had to do from there is negotiate a fair arrangement so he could feel comfortable giving me the fifteen automatons. After a week of going back and forth, we agreed that I would help him with some specific marketing in exchange for his collection.

I now own those automatons.

Later, once the deal was done, I asked him what made him change his mind about parting with the rare items.

"It was your story about your landlord," he explained. "That really got to me. I could easily imagine my friend who gave me the automatons being okay with me giving them to you but not selling them to you."

Hypnotic stories can work wonders. Whenever you want to persuade someone, consider telling a story about someone who did what you want the person you are persuading to do. The story can seep in easier than a direct command. And the results can be miraculous.

Look at me—I'm now surrounded by automatons. I'll soon be opening The Joe Vitale Museum of Automated Life and Other Curiosities.

As you can see, hypnotic stories are an important part of Hypnotic Writing.

35

HOW TO
CONTROL THE
"COMMAND CENTER"
IN YOUR
PROSPECT'S MIND

Here's a million-dollar secret I've never shared with anyone. When you use it, you will get inside your prospect's head and manipulate their thinking to get them to do what you want—including sending you money right now for your product or service. Sound hard to believe? Keep reading and I'll prove my point to you.

Right now, as you read these words, you are practicing the very thing I'm going to describe. Centuries ago people read books by moving their lips. Over time—and probably due to complaints from the family—people learned to close their mouths. But virtually all people still read the letters you send them by saying the words in their head, almost as if they were speaking them out loud, but in reality speaking only to themselves. You're probably doing it right now.

You are, aren't you? It doesn't reflect anything about your intelligence. It's how most of us read. I read more than most people and I still read the same way you do, "mouthing" the words in my head. It's how most of us humans accept the written word. Relax. You're normal.

Why is this important?

Because this is a way for you to plant hypnotic commands right into the skulls of people. This is staggering power. When people read your sales letter, you are, in essence, right *inside* the head of the very person you want to persuade. They are speaking your words—your commands, if you do this right—to themselves. You are in their "command center."

Think of the power you have!

Unless you've taken a speed reading course—which teaches you to scan pages and avoid seeing single words—you are like everyone else: hearing what I want you to hear right now, in your own mind. In reality, I'm in your head! What am I going to make you do? Buy my books? Hire me to write copy for you? Make you go out with me and do my bidding? Hmm.

You can imagine the kind of power this gives me and can give you once you learn how to do it, too. And that's what I give you a quick-start lesson in: how to control your prospect's mind.

First, accept that people are reading your sales letters (or ads, memos, e-mail, web copy, and so on) by pronouncing your words in their heads. This means you are in the "forbidden zone" and ready to rewire their brains.

Second, keep in mind that as people read, they think. You are doing it right now and you have been doing it throughout this chapter. You are talking to yourself as you read. You are thinking.

People read your words and also ask questions, as if you were there to answer them. Your job as a Hypnotic Writer is to anticipate those questions and answer them. Do so and people will follow your commands.

Are you with me? As I mentioned earlier, I've never discussed this concept before because I felt it was too damned powerful to release. But when Mark Joyner asked me to expand on the material in my best-selling *Hypnotic Writing* series of books, I figured I owed the man my ace in the hole.

Here it is and here's how it works:

Write your sales letter with all the Hypnotic Writing skills you have learned from this book. Use every trick you've learned to grab and hold attention, build desire, and lead to a strong close, because you know that's how you create truly Hypnotic Writing.

And *as* you write, ask yourself, "What is my reader thinking right now?" This is much like trying to handle objections in a traditional sales call. The difference is, you are doing this in writing. Your customer isn't standing in front of you. He or she may be thousands of miles away.

But that person is reading your words—voicing those words in their head—and that person is asking questions. Anticipate them and answer them and you will up the odds in creating a sales letter that easily persuades.

Let me explain this another way: Hypnotists know that you will obey their commands as long as you don't already have a counter-suggestion in mind to the contrary. They can tell you, "Go open the window," and you will do just that *unless* you have a counter-thought, such as "But it's cold outside" or "I don't have a good reason to open the window."

This same dynamic goes on inside your readers. You can tell them, "Send me money now for my new gizmo," and they will do exactly that *unless* they have counterthoughts (read: objections) in them. As you probably know, most of your readers will have counterthoughts. Your job is to anticipate them and answer them and *then* give your command.

I use this little-known hypnotic skill in all my sales letters.

I work hard to create a headline that relays a benefit in a curious way. I sweat to write an opening that yanks attention from wherever it was to my words. And then I use this "hypnotic dialogue process" to write the letter.

In other words, I write my letter while pretending to talk to one person about my product or service. In a real way, I'm talking to myself. As I talk on the page, I imagine what my prospect will ask next. It's a dialogue in my mind. But the truth is, that same dialogue will end up in my prospect's mind if I do this right. You've been doing it throughout this chapter. You've been reading my words and asking yourself questions. Right?

Throughout the writing of this chapter, I kept asking myself, "What will he ask?" By anticipating your questions, I could handle them in a persuasive way. I could, in short, lead you to my way of thinking and to doing what I want.

For example, right after my opening paragraph, I wrote, "Sound hard to believe?" I placed the question there because that's probably exactly where you *asked* the question in your own mind. You read my opening lines—about my big promise to show you how to get people to send you money—and inside yourself you said something like, "That's pretty hard to believe. Prove it."

And right there, right on cue, comes my question. I anticipated your thoughts and answered them by using the dialogue process. And what did I install in your mind while you were reading?

Go back through this chapter and see if you can find this "dialogue process" at work. And then notice what you do next, because that action will reflect the command I secretly embedded in you. And now that your objections are handled, you have little choice but to act on it, or not.

36

THE ONE HYPNOTIC COMMAND THAT ALWAYS WORKS

I learned about the one hypnotic command that always works from hypnotists. A good hypnotist will never give a subject a choice or offer a list of "reasons why you should fall asleep right now."

Instead, a good hypnotist will simply issue a command, "When I count to three, you will close your eyes" or "When I snap my fingers, you will bark like a dog." The subject responds because they want to please the hypnotist and because they don't have much of a choice.

Your prospects are nearly the same. Give them too many "reasons why you should buy" and you risk boring them, overwhelming them, or irking them. Give them the "one hypnotic command that always works" and they will do your bidding.

Want proof? Okay. Answer me this: Why are you reading this chapter?

I'm betting the title for this chapter promised you something you felt would be worth your reading to get. You want to know the one hypnotic command that always works so you can use it to increase sales, get more dates, or in some way get more of what you want from people. Right?

But note that I didn't have to tell you all those reasons to read this chapter. I gave you *one* sentence—the title to this piece—and you decided to read it based on it alone. Any further reasons for reading this were supplied by you, not me.

What you just did was illustrate the very point of this chapter. You are reading this for *one* reason. There may be subcategories to that one reason, but the bottom line is that you are here, absorbing these words, because I've promised you one main benefit: the hypnotic command that always works.

The trend with the best copywriters today is to pile on the reasons people should buy the product being offered and to give an avalanche of testimonials to prove others love the product. There is nothing wrong with this approach to creating sales letters that work as long as it *also* contains the one hypnotic command that works.

What I suggest here is that the hypnotic command alone—when done right—is so powerful that you may not even need that long list of reasons to buy. You could feasibly write a hypnotic headline and follow it with a story and end up with some terrific sales. (Believe me, I've done it!) I know this may be a radical thought, but stick with me.

Just what is this "one hypnotic command that always works"?

It depends on your audience. When I was considering writing this chapter, I asked myself "What is the one thing my readers will want to know?" Since I know many of you have read my two e-books on Hypnotic Writing, and you consider me a Hypnotic Writer, some deep insights into those subjects might intrigue you.

I further speculated that if I titled this piece "the *one* command that always works," you would subliminally know there is one very powerful thing to learn here. And of course, the "one" in the headline refers to the one thing I am trying to get across here. Follow?

Okay, okay. Here's my one point in a nutshell: Know the exact one thing your prospects want and tie everything you say to it.

Let me explain: If you are selling laundry soap, you might list numerous benefits and features, everything from "smells good" to "protects colors" to "gets out stains" to "cheaper than the other brands" to "works in cold or hot water" to who knows what. But what you want to focus on is the *one* thing that your laundry soap buyers want the most. Whatever that is, create your hypnotic command based on it.

In other words, if the one thing laundry soap buyers want is "allergy free soap," then pack all your Hypnotic Writing power into one line that says *that* is what they will get from your soap. Even *Allergy Free Soap Here* would work as a hypnotic line in that scenario. Anything else you say may be weak and even annoying compared to telling your prospects the one thing they want to hear.

Here's another example: Say you are selling a magic trick of some sort. You can list everything from "easy" to "new" to "inexpensive" to "amaze your friends" to "add it to your collection" to any number of possible selling statements.

But what is the *one* thing your audience of budding magicians wants? Whatever it is, focus on it. That will be the one hypnotic command that will explode sales. Since I am a magician, I know *Easily Amaze Your Friends* would be a great single hypnotic command for the magic audience. In fact, I know of one magic supplier who uses the slogan "Working hard to make you amazing." He's on the right track. He knows magicians want to be amazing, and he's got a hypnotic command to convey that message. He'll capture the right audience and get them itching to buy from that one line alone. Right about now you should be asking yourself "But how do I find out what the one thing is that my prospects want?"

Good question. The answer is to first ask them, and second, test them. In short, call, e-mail, and visit some people from your audience of prospects. Talk to them. Find out what the one thing is they want from your business. Too many bad copywriters just trust their hunches on what their audience wants. Don't do it. As much as I believe in intuition—after all, I wrote a book called *Spiritual Marketing*—the only way to know with any certainty what your prospects want is to question them.

But even that isn't good enough. After you question them, test them. Write ads, letters, and e-mail campaigns where your prospects' revealed "one desire" dominate. If you've truly hit on the one thing they want, sales will roll in. If you miss, try another "one desire" and see if that pulls better. Again, what you are looking for is the one hypnotic command that will make your prospects buy, buy, buy.

Now let me assure you that you might still give a long list of reasons why people should buy from you, *but* be sure that long list stems from your key "one hypnotic command." If you don't use the key command that activates the buying impulse in your prospects, your long list will be a grab bag of odds and ends that may confuse people. You need the one command to grab their attention and maybe even close the deal right there, yet you may still need your list of benefits to help convince them to buy. Don't dismiss your list. Just don't rely on it.

Finally, how do you write a hypnotic command?

That would take a book to explain. In short, write it the same way you do a good headline: short, engaging, relevant to your audience. Think of what your prospects want and give them one tight line that suggests you have it for them.

Look at the titles for articles in *Reader's Digest* magazine, for example. They are intriguing, short, and vibrant. Write your command the same way. And for motivation to get yourself to work at writing a hypnotic suggestion, remind yourself that it takes only one good line to make someone buy.

After all, my one hypnotic command got you to read this entire chapter, didn't it?

37

WHAT I LEARNED FROM *THE SEA WOLF*

One of the writers who deeply affected me growing up was Jack London. He's probably most famous for the book *The Call of the Wild*. But he wrote over 50 books. Some of them nonfiction. A few autobiographical. But by far most of them were great works of fiction. One of my favorites is *The Sea Wolf*.

One thing I learned from Jack London is to never . . .

Before I explain what I learned, let me point out that Jack London was a powerhouse writer. He wrote adventure tales packed with energy, conflict, and character. Whether the lead character was a person or an animal, you could always identify with them.

In *The Sea Wolf*, the lead character is the captain, called the sea wolf. He's mad. He's insane. And he's driving our narrator and everyone else batty as well.

But you get to know the captain through the book. You learn he's smart, well read, articulate, and a bit of a testosterone freak. But what could you expect when he came from the mind of Jack London, one of America's most popular he-man authors of the early part of the 1900s?

London himself was a sailor. He had spent time on the sea,

owned boats, wrote of his travels, and lived life to its fullest. One of my favorite quotes is this:

> **I would rather be ashes than dust!**
>
> **I would rather that my ashes should burn out in a brilliant blaze than it should be stifled by dry rot.**
>
> **I would rather be a superb meteor, every atom of me in magnificent glow, than a sleepy and permanent planet. The proper function of a man is to live, not to exist. I shall not waste my days trying to prolong them. I shall use my time.**
>
> **—Jack London**

No wonder he was dead by the age of 40. He lived a hard, active, wild life, and regretted none of it.

You can imagine my thrill when I went to the Jack London Ranch outside San Francisco at the end of 2000. I went to San Francisco to be interviewed on a new television show. While there, I rented a car and headed out to Jack London country.

I went to his famous home, too, called Wolf Mansion. I walked around what was left of it anyway. It had burned nearly completely to the ground before London ever got to move into it.

And I went to London's grave. He was cremated and put under one of the giant volcanic red boulders on his property.

I also went inside a museum on the property, now part of the California parks system, and saw an old movie with Jack London in it. It was, of course, a black and white film, a silent one, but Jack London's smile lit up the frames. It was incredible to see this hero of mine so obviously alive, to realize he had indeed once lived and walked the earth, just like you or me.

What I learned from Jack London's writing, and especially from *The Sea Wolf*, was to keep readers hooked by not giving them an ending to something you know they wanted to see resolved.

In other words, many of London's chapters end right when new conflict bubbles up. You have no recourse but to keep reading in order to resolve the tension London has created.

In essence, he has hypnotized you to keep reading.

I did the same thing at the beginning of this chapter.

When I said, "One thing I learned from Jack London is to never . . . ," I was setting you up for a lockdown in this chapter.

In short, I held your attention by not resolving the statement I had begun and had bet you wanted to hear the ending of.

And that's a secret to creating Hypnotic Selling Stories.

You have to keep your readers or listeners engaged. One way to do that is to tell them you're about to say something important— and then go into a new subject, with the promise that you'll return to the original one in a minute.

Believe me, it works every time.

It got you to read this entire chapter, didn't it?

38

YOUR TURNING POINT MESSAGE

Last night Nerissa and I watched the movie, *The Rookie*. We loved it. It's the inspiring true story of an older man who gets a chance to pursue his dream of playing major league baseball. It's a great movie.

The ads for the movie all say it's about going for your dreams. They're right. The movie certainly nudges you in that direction. But that's not all the movie has to offer.

Every movie—every book, play, article, sales pitch, or anything else that might be called a story—has what I call a turning point message. You can call it a TPM, for the sake of sounding cool.

A TPM is usually one line that causes the story to almost completely turn around. It might seem like the motto of the movie. Or the main message of the story. Or even just a mental stumper to get you to think. It will often feel like the philosophical foundation for the entire story.

A TPM is the central message of the story that causes the lead character to rethink what he or she is doing, or even to cause you, the witness to the story, to rethink what you are doing.

It's usually given at the point of dramatic transformation, when the entire plot changes or the main character changes.

Last night, while watching *The Rookie*, we heard the TPM two-thirds of the way through the story. The main character has a chance to pursue his dream of playing baseball again. He's troubled. He doesn't know what to do. Does he leave his family and his job and go on the road playing ball again? He goes to his father, whom he has a strained relationship with, to get advice. That's when you hear the TPM.

The character's father says, "It's fine to do what you want to do, but sooner or later you have to do what you were meant to do."

There it is. It's the turning point in the movie. It's the line that makes the character angry at first. And it's the line that stayed with Nerissa and me long after the movie had ended. We even talked about it over breakfast this morning.

Every Hypnotic Selling Story has a TPM.

Take the movie *Good Will Hunting*, another one of my all-time favorite films. The TPM in it occurs when the troubled youth hears his counselor repeatedly tell him, "It's not your fault—It's not your fault—It's not your fault."

Without a TPM, a story lacks heart. Your story might have character, conflict, and even humor. But without the TPM, it lacks a core that will make it unforgettable.

Let's say you are creating a story about how someone used your product or service and made a difference in their lives. Any story will do. You might even tell about your own experience with your product or service.

But add a TPM and your story will plant itself in your reader's or listener's mind and virtually never disappear.

Take this very chapter. It, too, is a story. I told you about watching the movie, *The Rookie*. I told you about watching *Good Will Hunting*, too. And I told you I believe all truly Hypnotic Selling Stories have a TPM in them.

Well, what's the TPM in what I've said here? Think about it for a second.

I think it is when I said, "Your story might have character, conflict, and even humor. But without the TPM, it lacks a core that will make it unforgettable." That, to me, is the turning point message in this very chapter.

I'm telling you about the need for a TPM to help you create hypnotic stories that sell people.

How do you create a TPM?

You don't. You let them evolve from the telling of your story.

The trick is to *let* them evolve. Don't try to control them. When you do, you kill them.

In other words, don't be too ruthless in how you edit your stories. It's tempting to take out all of the lines that I said are TPMs. But if I had, the essence of this chapter would be gone.

Think about that before going to the next chapter.

39

WHAT EVERYONE
WILL ALWAYS READ

I had a fight this morning with my neighbor.

We don't fight often, but sometimes it happens. What can I say? We're human. Fights happen.

And that's good news. It's good news because it's the number one thing people love to read about. Give me a conflict and I'll give you a story. It's that simple.

Think about it. What are the best movies about? What are the best books about? Don't they always involve someone who wants something and is struggling to get it? Isn't something in his or her way? In short, there's always a conflict.

Conflicts make great news, too. Any time two people fight, or two groups, or two armies, the media will be there. Why? Because conflict is, at heart, hypnotic.

You can use this to your advantage. The next time you want to create a Hypnotic Selling Story, look for a conflict. The conflict can be between you and another person, two other people, or even ideas that are butting heads.

For example, I began this chapter with the phrase, "I had a fight this morning with my neighbor."

I did that for one main reason: to get your attention.

I knew your hardwired human interest in battle would make you at least curious about my opening line. From there, I wove a story about how we humans crave conflict, and how you can use that fact to create stories no one can resist.

The truth is, I did not have a fight with my neighbor. I live in the Hill Country outside Austin, Texas. I don't even know my neighbors.

But by beginning this chapter with the hint of a conflict, I got your attention and got you to read all of this.

See how it works?

40

YOUR CONNOTATION IS SHOWING

When I was in junior high school, I recall my English professor telling me about the denotation and connotation of words. Denotations are the dictionary meanings. Connotations are the colloquial meanings. If you didn't know both, you could confuse people.

For example, there are 18 denotations for the word *great*. (Check your dictionary.)

But the connotation of the same word means much more. Haven't you used it to mean everything from "I loved it!" to "It was incredible" to "It was better than I thought"?

In fact, the word *great* is so often used that it's almost meaningless. We simply assume anyone who says something was great means they liked it. Maybe a little. Maybe a lot. But they mean something positive. That's the general acceptance of the word *great*. That's the connotation of the word.

Well, stories are the same way.

Stories have a direct meaning—most likely what you are describing or declaring.

But stories also have an indirect meaning—what people conclude from what you are describing or declaring.

In short, stories have denotations as well as connotations.

Hypnotic Selling Stories are created around their connotations. In other words, their indirect communications do the selling more than their direct communications.

I'm sure you'd like an example by now.

One day many years ago I met a woman at a restaurant in Houston. I was teaching writing classes at the time. She wanted to meet me to ask questions about my classes, my books, and so forth. At that time, I didn't mind meeting complete strangers for an hour of lively discussion.

I told her about classes and said something along these lines:

"I love teaching my classes. People always buy my books and tapes after it ends, too. My first e-book *Hypnotic Writing* sells the best. I'm not sure what gets people so excited about it but they line up to buy it. Several people wrote books of their own after reading it. I make $40 every time I sell it, so I'm smiling in class the whole time."

After a few minutes of my impassioned talk, she smiled and said, "You do it so well."

"I do what so well?" I asked.

"You're selling me on your books without asking me to buy them," she explained. "I want all of them."

That's when I realized I had created a Hypnotic Selling Story.

My exact dialogue was simply the denotation of my communication. But my connotation said things like "My books are great" and "People use them for quick results" and "Joe's classes are popular."

Do you see what I mean?

Here's another quick story.

Nerissa came up to my office earlier today and asked for my help with a classified ad she wanted to run. She owns a rental unit in Austin and wants a new tenant. So we went over the various words she could use in her ad. We also went online and noted all the other similar ads running for places like hers. It was clear she had to word her ad differently.

I suggested she begin her ad with a question. Since all the other ads simple declared, "Great location!" or "Great view!" she needed to stand out from the crowd. So we went with: "Do you like walking, hiking, or just watching trees and birds?" She liked the headline and used it in her ad.

What did you notice?

On the denotation level, the message is along the lines of just the facts: I helped Nerissa by creating a unique headline for her.

But on the connotation level the communication is more like, "If you want an ad written, call Joe. Even his girlfriend goes to him in a pinch."

When you create your own Hypnotic Selling Stories, keep in mind there are two messages being communicated: the direct one and the indirect one.

The first should hold the attention of people.
The second should sell them.

In fact, this entire chapter has a denotation and a connotation.
The denotation is that every story has two meanings.
What is the connotation?

(Hint: It's whatever you concluded from the chapter. There is no right or wrong answer.)

My friend Blair Warren, author of the powerful book *The Forbidden Keys to Persuasion*, says this:

"One reason stories are so persuasive is that they allow people to draw their own conclusions. Ironically, the conclusion drawn must be based on the material as presented in the story—material placed there by the storyteller. Thus, the lesson for persuasion is, tell a story that doesn't "ram a conclusion down your audience's throat," but one that naturally leads your audience to make the conclusion that supports your proposition. As the following excerpt explains, people rarely argue with their own conclusions, making an effective story a virtual Trojan horse for the persuader's ideas.

"I remember reading a story many years ago about Ted Turner. Though I can't recall the author, the title, the magazine, or anything substantive about the article, there was something about it I will never forget. In it, there was a very brief account of the author riding along in Turner's vehicle as they got to know one another. At one point, Turner unexpectedly stopped his vehicle and, without saying a word, walked over to a soda can lying on the ground. He picked it up, threw it into the back of his vehicle, and continued driving. With that single anecdote the author painted a picture of an environmentally friendly and conscientious man. Had he simply said those things about Turner, they'd have gone unnoticed. But by showing Turner in action, the author allowed me to make that conclusion on my own. And not only have I never forgotten it, I've never questioned it.

"Without a doubt, we are more committed to what we conclude than what we are told. If we come to believe something is false, virtually nothing will convince us it is true. If we come to believe something is true, virtually nothing will convince us it is false. The problem is, despite our faith in our conclusions, they often lead us astray without us even being aware of it. While few of us give this a second thought, masters of persuasion never lose sight of the fact that people sometimes believe what they are told, but never doubt what they conclude."

Again, keep these ideas in mind as you move through this book and consider writing your own Hypnotic Selling Stories.

As you can imagine, you're dealing with phenomenal power here. Use it wisely.

41

WHAT ARE MY SECRETS FOR WRITING HYPNOTIC SELLING STORIES?

What did you notice about the title of this chapter?
I asked you a question, didn't I?

In fact, I just asked two more questions.

(I'm tempted to add, "Didn't I?")

I have found questions to be a remarkable way to engage people, to get them started reading your story. As my friend Joe Sugarman says, the goal of the first line of any sales story is to get people to read the next line. Well, when I use a question as my first line, I'm virtually guaranteed to get you to read the next line.

You're still reading, aren't you?

(Yes, that was another question.)

Now that you're near the end of the first section of this book, I reveal one of my favorite secrets for writing Hypnotic Selling Stories.

Yes, I'm talking about questions. I love questions. But unless the question is open-ended, there's the risk it will not engage your reader or listener.

In other words, if the title of this chapter was something like: Do You Know My Secrets for Writing Hypnotic Selling Stories?, you could answer it with a yes or a no and all would be over. You wouldn't have much reason to keep reading. That's not good.

Instead, by asking an open-ended question as: What Are My Secrets for Writing Hypnotic Selling Stories?, there is no way you can accurately answer it without reading this chapter.

Do you see how powerful this technique is? (Yes, that was another question.)

So my tip to you is to remember to engage people with questions. The more open-ended, the better.

Got it?

42

HYPNOTIC BLOGGING

M ost people write boring blogs. I almost didn't start my own at http://www.mrfireblog.com because I was disgusted by all the self-indulgent blogs on the Internet.

But then I thought, what if I used Hypnotic Writing on my blog? By doing so, I could make my blog stand out in the crowd. The idea worked. People who didn't normally spend more than one minute on a blog would visit mine and end up spending hours there, fascinated by what they were reading.

Here's how I used a hypnotic story on one of my blog posts:

How Lindsay Lohan and I Discovered the Fountain of Youth or The Psychology of the Second Interest

Last night I dreamed I went on a quest into a dark jungle to find The Secret www.whatisthesecret.tv to health, wealth, and happiness.

When I returned from my travels, glad to get to my tent, tired but excited by what I had dug up, famous singer/actress/model Lindsay Lohan was waiting for me.

I was a little surprised, but I just figured I attracted her. (See www.attractorfactor.com.)

After all, *7th Heaven* actress Jessica Biel loves my book *The Attractor Factor* and actor James Caan accepted my book when he and I hung out together on the set of *Las Vegas*. (See http://www.mrfire.com/photogallery.html.)

So having Lindsay Lohan in my tent wasn't *too* surprising.

So I said hey.

She wanted to hear about my trip into the wilds. She seemed excited and fascinated, her hypnotic eyes locked on mine as I told her my tale.

I told her that weeks earlier I stumbled across a rare plant that could be turned into a tea that helped people start *youthing* rather than aging.

Despite her young age, and her wealth, and her fame, she was smart enough to know this could be a huge moneymaker.

She wanted to know more.

I reached for my dirty burlap bag and pulled out the root of the plant I had found.

She sensed this was something historic.

"This will help people lose weight and grow younger?" she asked.

"I'm sure of it," I said. "Look at me. Don't I look younger already?"

She stared at me as if I were a talking car, but she nodded.

"You look *great!*" she said.

Nothing like having a sexy movie star compliment you.

She added, "You won't even need to bribe people to *buy this stuff* like you did at www.themotherofallbribes.com."

"I'm not so sure," I told her. "People don't take action unless they are motivated to do so. An ethical bribe gets them to get off their butts. They may not even buy the Fountain of Youth in a bottle without some added incentive. We in marketing call it **The Psychology of the Second Interest.**

I explained to her that even though my latest book *Life's Missing Instruction Manual* is good for people, they won't *buy it right now* unless something extra moves them to do so.

That's why I'm offering more than $13,000 in bonuses when people get the book at www.lifesmissingmanual.com.

And it's that very bribe that caused my book to rocket to #1 at Amazon and stay there for *four days*.

It's still a top bestseller right now.

Lindsay seemed impressed.

She moved closer to me.

I held my breath, not sure what she wanted.

"Joe, can I ask you a question?" she seductively whispered, almost like one of her songs on her new music CD www.lindsaylohanmusic.com.

"Ah . . . er . . . yes," I replied, stiffening.

I wasn't sure *what* she was going to ask.

Finally, she spoke: "Can I go with you on your next trip into the jungle?"

Hmmm. Lindsay Lohan wants to put on a backpack and take a trip into the darkness of the forest with me.

What should I say?

I know what my beautiful Nerissa would *want* me to say.

That's about when I woke up.

If I were a student of Jung or Freud and better understood dream interpretation (http://www.dreammoods.com/), I might know what this dream was really trying to tell me.

Do *you* have any idea?

Ao Akua,

Joe

www.mrfire.com; www.HypnoticMarketingInc.com

P.S. Despite what you might be thinking about hypnotic stories, hypnotic language, and other hypnotic secret things found in www.HypnoticWritingWizard.com, the above was a dream I *really* had last night. I'm not making it up. Really.

P.P.S. I wonder if Lindsay Lohan had the same dream? In one of her songs the lyrics *could* be speaking about me: "I can't live without you . . . Can't breathe without you . . . I dream about you . . ." http://www.metrolyrics.com/lyrics/2144148763/Lindsay_Lohan/Over

As you can see, the story is embedded with hypnotic commands, some obvious, some not so obvious. How many of them did you spot?

Let's start with the headline. The original headline, when I wrote the first draft of the blog, was My Dream of Lindsay Lohan. I didn't stop there because I didn't think anyone would care about my dream. I needed to make it more hypnotic. That's when I decided to make the headline about a mystery, on how she and I discovered the fountain of youth.

You might also note that the word *discover* in the headline is a hypnotic word. And the lead word *How* suggests something being solved. I didn't stop there, because I added a secondary headline. The idea of The Psychology of the Second Interest sounds curious, which of course is a powerful hypnotic tool.

The blog post then picks up with the actual story. As you read it, you can see in your mind the events unfold. On the blog, I placed an actual picture of Lindsay Lohan, which helped people pay attention to my writing. (She's pretty hypnotic to look at.) But the story itself keeps people riveted.

You should also notice that I use dialogue in the story. This is a hypnotic method used by every great author from Agatha Christie to, well, me. Anything with quotation marks around it is unconsciously perceived as being alive, interesting, and happening right now. We learned to pay attention to quotes because they are usually around something interesting. I use them to keep people riveted.

As you read the post carefully, you should notice embedded commands. For example, when I wrote, "She added, 'You won't even need to bribe people to *buy this stuff* like you did at www .themotherofallbribes.com,' " I used the command *buy this stuff* to command people to actually *buy this stuff*.

I suggest you study the post for any other elements of Hypnotic Writing at work. And for further study, visit my blog at www.mrfire.com.

Here's an example of a hypnotic story in an e-mail:

I didn't know who "Mr. H" was. Not until he got in his jet two years ago and flew down to see me.

Even then all I knew was that he is a wealthy businessman who started a simple business in his basement and now makes around $12,000,000 a year.

He read one of my books, liked it, and asked to visit with me.

He flew down, stayed the night with us, and told us his whole story.

I was fascinated.

That's when he told me he was the mysterious "Mr. H" who had been recorded years earlier revealing his secrets.

That's when he explained how he turned a dumb looking web site into an "ATM machine" that makes $32,876 a day.

As you can imagine, there's lots to learn about marketing and success from this "Mr. H" character.

And now you can learn his secrets.

Those long lost audios are now available again. I suggest you take a look. See http://www.1shoppingcart.com/app/?Clk= 1338171.

He'll probably never fly down to visit you, and he may never fly back to visit me again (I don't think he liked what we fed him), but here's your chance to hear his wisdom whenever you want it. If I were you, I'd get it now, before these audios once again disappear.

Go see.

Joe

P.S. What Is Beyond Marketing?
See http://www.mrfireblog.com.

Here's another example of an e-mail using the hypnotic story approach.

Look in the mirror.

Can you tell what your cholesterol level is?

I couldn't either by just looking at myself.

So I had blood work done. To my surprise, it revealed that mine is high.

I couldn't believe it.

Not only am I in good shape, had just lost 80 pounds, work out every day, and eat right (I think), but I feel fine.

That's the trouble with cholesterol: You can't feel if it's high or low. It's a tricky devil.

I grew concerned about mine. I researched online but got confused with all the promises of lowered cholesterol with questionable pills, some natural, some prescribed.

What was I to do?

I called a friend of mine who is a medical doctor and an emergency room physician.

He told me there is a natural product that lowers cholesterol in 30 days by about 30%.

All you have to do is take two capsules at dinner.

That's it.

He's so confident it will work for anyone that he says to take your blood work now, and then take it after 30 days of using his formula. He says your cholesterol *will* be lower.

I wanted a bottle.

But he didn't have any.

It's his formula, but he's sold out. Since he's a start up company, he was waiting to create the next batch.

I didn't want to wait.

I offered to pay for his new batch.

"But it's $12,500," he said.

"I'll pay it," I said.

I became an investor on the spot.

But all I really wanted was the bottle.

In short, I'm paying $12,500 for a bottle of capsules that will help lower my cholesterol—naturally and safely—and within 30 days.

The good news for you—or for anyone you know with high cholesterol—is you can now get a bottle for only $22.

Because I made an investment of $12,500, there is now a limited supply of bottles for you to get for yourself or family or friends.

If I were you, I'd do it.

Look in the mirror again.

Don't you deserve to be healthy?

See www.CardioSecret.com.

Go for it.

Joe

P.S. The formula contains a secret ingredient that, as far as I know, no other capsule contains. Yet this secret ingredient can prevent heart attacks and strokes, while also lowering cholesterol. You can get a Special Report on this at http://www.CardioSecret.com.

Stories are powerful for another reason, too. The following chapter might be considered Advanced Hypnotic Writing, but I want to discuss it to give you a sense of the power you hold in your hands when you create a sales letter or a web site with hypnotic stories and Hypnotic Writing.

43

REMINDERS AS TRIGGERS

Have you ever truly analyzed a conversation? What typically happens is someone talks to you about an event in their life. They are sharing their story.

That's simple enough. But what happens next is you look through your memory banks for something similar to what you just heard. You might then say, "Something like that happened to me once, too!" And then you take your turn in the conversation.

As the person listens to you, they are doing the same thing. They might even get so excited when a thought or memory occurs to them, that they interrupt you and tell their next story.

What is happening here?

Roger Schank, writing in *Tell Me a Story*, says, "The question to think about is how, after someone says something to you in conversation, something comes to mind to say back. Even the simplest of responses have to be found somewhere in memory."

In short, stories contain elements—usually specific words—that *trigger* memories in people. When I tell you about my experience of having lunch today, and mention that an attractive young blonde-haired woman waited on me and seemed to flirt with me, I am setting you up to drift off, mentally, from the conversation.

The word *lunch* might remind you that you haven't eaten yet, and now suddenly you're thinking about food. Or my mention of the attractive young woman might remind you of sex, and suddenly your mind is off in a naughty place.

Where *did* your mind go, anyway?

Again, stories contain triggers. Schank calls them "reminders." These triggers are reminders of previous thoughts. Those triggers will cause people to mentally drift into an imagery experience that may or may not serve you.

If you want people thinking about food, mention lunch. If you want people thinking about sex, mention the attractive young woman. But also be aware of what is happening here. Your words are causing activity in the other person's mind.

This is what happens when anyone has a conversation. One sentence said by one person leads to a reminder in the other person, which leads to their saying something. The next person then hears a reminder and makes their statement. Two people in rapport and talking a mile a minute are two people experiencing reminders.

All of this is good news for you and your Hypnotic Writing. You want to consciously control your visitor's mental experience through your Hypnotic Writing. Again, use stories to convey your message. But keep in mind that the words you use within those stories will trigger reminders.

You want people thinking of you in a positive way, so refrain from any negative reminders. Keep people focused on what they get from your product or service, and keep them focused with a story that reminds them of their wants.

As you read this book, you will start to remember stories that have influenced you.

But what about just transforming your existing copy into Hypnotic Writing? How do you take your existing sentences and add to them or actually rewrite them to give them more power? How do you do *that*?

Well, let's see.

44

How to
Change Average
Writing into
Hypnotic Writing

L et me tell you a secret. As I mentioned earlier in this book, whenever someone hires me to rewrite their sales materials, I run a Copy Translation Service in my head. What I do is read each sentence of their site as though it were written in a foreign language. The foreign language is Ego Copy. It was written by the person who owns the company and is usually full of fluff. What I do is translate that Ego Copy into Reader Copy. That means I take their line and turn it into a line that speaks to the reader's interest. An example might help.

Nearly every sales letter you read will contain a *we* statement. It's usually something like "We have been in business five years" or "We love to make donuts" (or whatever they make).

All of those are Ego Copy statements. That's a foreign language to your readers. It doesn't appeal to them at all.

What I do is translate those Ego Statements into Reader Benefits or Reader Copy. I might turn "We have been in business five years" to "You can rest assured you will get your item from us on time and to your satisfaction, as we've been doing this over five years."

And I might turn: "We love to make donuts" to "You'll love our mouthwatering donuts because our passion for making them energizes every one we create for you."

Do you see the difference?

Most writing focuses on the person who did the writing. What you want to do is focus on the interests of the person reading your words. In short, get out of your ego and into the reader's ego. Speak to *their* interests.

Let's look at some basic tips on how to transform your current words into Hypnotic Writing. The following are excerpts from my e-book *The Hypnotic Writing Swipe File*, which you can learn more about at http://www.HypnoticWritingSwipeFile.com.

31 Hypnotic Headline Words

You can generate headlines for your sales copy fast simply by using words from this list. Simply take the following words, add them to your product or service, claim or guarantee, and watch how easy it is to write a hypnotic headline.

> *announcing astonishing at last exciting exclusive fantastic fascinating first free guaranteed incredible initial improved love limited offer powerful phenomenal revealing revolutionary special successful super time-sensitive unique urgent wonderful you breakthrough introducing new how-to*

Announcing: Astonishing Guaranteed Free New Way to Find Love Now!

And since we're on the subject of headlines, let me state that marketing gurus and other peers of mine are finding that when they remove the banner at the top of their web site, they get twice as many sales. Get that: *Twice as many sales!!*

Why? It seems that the banner distracts from what really does the engaging and the selling: the headline.

Again, what sells—what motivates people to take action—are words.

45

---

30 WAYS TO WRITE A
HYPNOTIC HEADLINE

Here's one of my biggest secrets: I write the headline first. It becomes an anchor for my entire message. It sums up what I want to say, holds my own passion, and builds curiosity. I may change my headline later, but I always begin with a working headline to get the steam going.

The following 30 ways to write a headline are worth gold. I spent years researching all the ways you could write a headline, and then created this set of 30 templates. This will make headline writing a snap for you.

You will need at least one main headline on your sales letter or web site. But you'll also need headlines throughout the body of your writing. These subheadlines help convey your message, keep people interested, and continue to build desire.

You'll also find that because there are three kinds of readers—word-for-worders, skimmers, and jumpers—you need subheadlines to appeal to all of them. So when you look through the following list, feel free to create as many headlines as you can for your product or service. You may need them all.

Headlines will make or break your ads. John Caples said a good headline can pull up to *19 times* better results for the same ad. Advertising pioneer James Webb said a top headline can bring in as much as *50 percent more* inquiries and sales. Ad genius David

Ogilvy said five times more people will read your headlines than will read your whole ad. "We pick out what we wish to read by headlines," wrote Claude Hopkins, arguably the greatest advertising man in history, in his famous book *Scientific Advertising*.

Often a headline is all a reader will glance at—and I do mean *glance* at—before rushing through the rest of the newspaper or on to the next web site. On average, most people will spend only *four seconds* per page! If your headline does not catch, trip, and stop your audience, you have lost them and you have lost a sale!

Here are 30 surefire ways to create a terrific hypnotic headline or improve an existing one.

1. Lead with these opening words.
   At Last!
   Announcing!
   New!

   Note the hint of excitement and "news" in the above words. *New* is hypnotic. Other good opening words include *introducing* and *finally*. Legally you can use only the word *new* if your product has been developed or improved within the past six months. If you have just invented a new device, certainly let the world know.

2. Round up your audience.
   Plumbers!
   Housewives!
   Sore Feet?

   This type of headline is "calling in" your target audience. If you are selling a book for lawyers, you might open by saying "Attention, lawyers!" With this approach you are certain to get the ear of the exact crowd you want. In hypnosis, getting attention is the first step to the trance state.

3. Promise a benefit.
   Free from Backache in 10 Minutes!
   Buy One Shirt—Get the Second free!
   Land a Job in 2 Days with New Method!

Benefits are why people buy. Decaffeinated coffee is a feature; *Lets you sleep better* is a benefit. If people have a back problem, they do not want to buy a pill; they want to buy relief from their pain. Free with relief from their pain. *Free from Backache in 10 Minutes,* tells them a cure is available. Sell the relief, not the prevention. When you speak about what people get, you capture their attention hypnotically.

4. Make it newsworthy.
   Major Breakthrough in Car Safety
   New Formula Restores Hair
   Seven "Lost Secrets" Discovered

   People devour news. Reveal the newsworthiness of your product or service and you will get attention. A new product is news. An old product with new uses is news. Arm & Hammer baking soda (which also started as a small business) has been around for decades, but the company keeps thinking of new ways for us to use its product—from brushing our teeth to putting it in the fridge to eliminate odors—and *that's* news. Again, anything new captivates interest, which is the beginning of hypnosis.

5. Offer something free.
   Free to Writers!
   Free Report Explains Tax Loopholes
   Free Book on Car Repairs

   Your free item has to be appropriate to the audience you are after. It may be free, but if they are not interested in it, they will not write or call you. Also, your free item has to be *really* free—with no catches or conditions—for you to be legally safe. Any small business can create a free item that is relevant.

6. Ask an intriguing question.
   What Are the Seven Secrets to Success?
   Do You Make These Mistakes in English?
   Which Gas Filter Will Boost Your Car's Performance?

Questions are a powerful way to involve readers. But your question has to be an open-ended one that hints of a benefit. If you ask a question that can be easily answered with a yes or no, you run the risk that your readers will not look beyond the question. But if your question is intriguing, it will pull readers into your copy to learn the answer. This is my favorite method for inducing a trance state.

7. Lead with a testimonial.
   "This is the most powerful weapon I've ever seen!" (Clint Eastwood)
   "These two books made me the wealthiest man alive." (Malcolm Forbes)
   "Here's why my race cars beat all others." (Mark Weisser)

   There is something about quotation marks that captures people's eyes. If your quote is intriguing (as are these fictional ones), they will force readers to read your copy. (Always use real testimonials from real people and always get their permission first.) Anyone who has ever used your product or service can give you a testimonial. And headlines put in quotes will get more attention—dialogue has life, and that attracts people.

8. Create a "how to" headline.
   How to Get Your Kids to Listen
   How to Tell When Your Car Needs a Tune-Up
   How to Win Friends and Influence People

   Because people want information, they are easily drawn to "how to" headlines that promise a benefit they are interested in. If you are selling washing machines, you might conjure up the headline, *How to Pick the Right Washing Machine for Your Needs.* You can add sparkle to virtually any headline by adding the word *how.* For example, *I Cut Hair* is a weak headline, but *How I Cut Hair* is more interesting. The "how to" is like a hypnotic command that brings people into your writing.

9. Quiz your readers.

How Smart Are You? Take This Quiz and See!
What Is Your Networking IQ?
Are You Qualified for Success?

People love quizzes. Use a question headline and then let the body of your ad be a quiz. For the ad to work, of course, it all has to tie in to what you are selling. The ad about your networking IQ, for example, is selling a book called *Power Networking*. If you are running a mechanic's shop, you might ask, *Is Your Car Healthy? Take This Quiz and See!* Your whole attempt is to somehow *involve* readers with your ad. A quiz is one way to do that. Involvement is how hypnosis begins and deepens.

10. Use the words these and why in your headline.

These Boats Never Sink
Why Our Dogs Cost More
Why These Skis Are Called "Perfect"

When you use the words *these* and *why* in your headline, you tend to create an attention-grabbing statement that will draw readers into the rest of your ad or sales letter. If you just said, "Our skis are perfect," few would be interested. But when you say, "*Why* these skis are called perfect," you generate curiosity—one of the most powerful motivators around. Simply add the word *why* to an existing headline to make it more engaging. *Buy Plumbing Supplies Here* is boring but *Why People Buy Plumbing Supplies Here* is interesting.

11. Use I and me headlines.

They Laughed When I Sat Down at the Piano—But When I Started to Play!
I Finally Discovered the Secret to Easy Writing!
Everywhere I Stick My Nose I Make Money

First-person headlines will work if they generate enough curiosity and hold a benefit. Everyone interested in playing the piano, for example, will be drawn to the first headline (one of the most successful headlines in history). *You* and *yours* in a headline do not always work because they signal a selling message and people become defensive. However *I* and *me* in a headline can deliver a selling message in a palatable way. Here's a good example: *I Wanted to Help People So Here's Why I Opened My Own Insurance Agency!* **Note:** Don't miss the *you* approach, either. After all, people will go into a hypnotic trance when you address *their* interests, not yours.

12. Put your product name in your headline.
    How Gymco Vitamins Make Runners Lightning Fast
    The Fiskin Ladder Saved My Husband's Life
    Thoughtline Helped Me Discover the Secret to Easy Writing

    How to Cure Warts is good, but *How Vitalism Cures Warts* is better. Since not everyone will stop and read your ad, putting your company name in the headline helps deliver some of your message. But do not make your company name the *focus* of your headline. Instead, write a riveting headline and slip your name into it. This approach plants a hypnotic seed in the mind of the reader.

13. Use the word *wanted*.
    Wanted—Nervous People
    Wanted—Safe Men for Dangerous Times
    Wanted—Executives Ready for Sudden Profits

    Wanted is a word loaded with curiosity. Lead with it and people are compelled to find out why you want nervous people (maybe for a seminar on overcoming fear) or why you want executives (maybe to offer them your new management program). Be sure to ask for the target audience you want. If you are offering something to attorneys, you might write a headline that begins *Wanted—Attorneys*. The word *wanted* is a hypnotic attention-getting word.

14. Use the word *breakthrough* in your headline.
    A Breakthrough in Alarm Systems
    Doctor Offers Breakthrough Hair Loss Formula
    Wanted—Attorneys Ready for Breakthrough Success

    Breakthrough implies news. It suggests that your product or service beats all other existing systems. A similar impact can be obtained with *record breaking* or *revolutionary*.

15. Set your headline in upper and lower case.
    HEADLINES IN ALL CAPS ARE HARD TO READ
    Headlines in Upper and Lower Case Are Easy to Read
    Got it?

    If people have to work to read your ad or sales letter or web site, they will awaken from their potential trance and stop reading.

16. Use as many words as you need.
    It Floats!
    How Often Do You Hear Yourself Saying, "No, I haven't read it; I've been meaning to!"
    Who Else Wants Beautiful Furniture?

    Headlines can be long or short. As long as they get the attention of your appropriate audience, arouse curiosity, and encourage people to read your ad, any length goes. You do not want to waste words, of course. But you do not need to limit yourself, either.

17. Feature your offer.
    Arrow Shirts at 50% Off
    Oil Change Special
    Join for Six Months—Get Next Six Months Free

    You have to be clear about the uniqueness of what you are selling for this to work. What are you offering that is head and shoulders above your competition? Focus on that.

18. Ask "who else?"

    Who Else Wants to Write a Book?
    Who Else Used to Say Singing Was Hard?
    Who Else Wants a Fail-Safe Burglar Alarm?

    Who else is an involving set of hypnotic words. It suggests that someone else got what you are offering and that it is possible for the reader to achieve or have it, too.

19. Use a guarantee.

    Guaranteed No-Stains-Ever Rug!
    Guaranteed to Go through Ice, Mud, or Snow—or We Pay the Tow!

    We live in the age of skepticism. Your offer should always run with a guarantee. But if you can say in the headline your offer is guaranteed, it will help to convince readers to look at your entire ad.

20. Admit a weakness.

    We're Number Two. We Try Harder.
    This Chef Makes Everything Except Salads!

    You will gain credibility if you confess you are not perfect. Too many ads and letters claim to be the magic bullet to all your ills. That is not believable. If you say you are *almost* a magic bullet, people will tend to believe the rest of your claims. In order to put people into a hypnotic trance, they must trust you.

21. Focus on positive end results.

    Whiter Teeth in 10 Days
    35 Pounds Slimmer in 30 Days

    Do not paint a negative picture thinking you will make a sale. People buy hopes and dreams. Do not sell "fat loss," instead sell "Almost Perfect Health!" Do not try to scare people into buying toothpaste by yelling, *Yellow Teeth Are Ugly!*, but instead sell the end result people want: *Whiter Teeth!* Again, people buy cures. But be believable. If your headline sounds like a stretch, people will not trust you. *35 Pounds Slimmer in 30 Days* is believable; *35 Pounds Slimmer Overnight* is not.

22. Warn your audience.

    WARNING to Doctors!
    Warning: Do Your Kids Play This Stereo?
    Small Business Owners Be Warned!

    You can grab your target audience with a warning to them. A warning promises information and invokes curiosity, both powerful hypnotic inducers.

23. Be careful with humor.

    Not everyone has a sense of humor, not everyone agrees on what is funny, and few people buy because of a joke. A slogan in advertising is "People don't buy from clowns." Small businesses that attempt to sell people with their humor usually flop. Why? You are not selling humor, you are selling your product or service. Do you want people to laugh or buy? If you insist on trying humor, try to make the punch line the same as your sales message. Here is an example: *Used Car Prices So Low It Hertz.*

24. Make it easy.

    Plumbing Problems Cured Easily
    Easy Way to Stop Roof Leaks

    People want results fast and easy. If you or your product can make their lives easier, say so.

25. Be careful with reverse type.

    You can use reverse type (white letters on a black background) for your headline but *do not* use reverse type for the rest of your ad or web site or sales letter. Too much reverse type is far too difficult for people to read. Using it in a headline, however, can increase the number of people who will see the ad.

26. Dramatize the benefit.

    Stop Sleeping like a Sardine! Now Sleep like a King!
    "Sound Pillow" Lets You Sleep with Neil Diamond!

People want action. They crave it. Show the excitement your product or service can give by dramatizing the benefits. A headline for large beds that reads *King Size Beds Are Roomy* is boring, but *Stop Sleeping like a Sardine! Now Sleep like a King!* is almost impossible to avoid. Drama is hypnotic.

27. Use proven clichés.

    JUST ARRIVED—New Accounting Method!
    ADVICE to Homeowners!
    THE TRUTH ABOUT Shoe Repair

    David Ogilvy, in *Confessions of an Advertising Man*, lists the following as proven headline clichés:

Free	Revolutionary
New	Startling
How to	Miracle
Suddenly	Magic
Now	Offer
Announcing	Quick
Introducing	Easy
It's Here	Wanted
Just Arrived	Challenge
Important Development	Advice to
Improvement	The Truth about
Amazing	Bargain
Compare	Hurry
Sensational	Last Chance
Remarkable	

    Ogilvy also says you can strengthen a headline by adding emotional words, such as, *Darling, Love, Fear, Proud, Friend,* and *Baby*.

28. Reveal a hidden benefit.

    How to Get Enthusiastic Applause—Even a Standing Ovation—Every Time You Speak

    This headline by Ted Nicholas sold a publication for speakers. One of the hidden or side benefits of reading the publication is learning how to get a standing ovation—something every speaker wants. Try to reveal the hidden benefit in your small business. Ask yourself: "What will people get as a result of using my product or service?"

29. Give reasons.

Three Reasons Why You Should Write a Book
Seven Reasons to Call This Doctor Today
Nine Reasons to Use This Maid Service

Reasons involve readers with your ad. To learn more, they have to read the rest of your copy. The trick to making this work is in targeting your prospects. If you are an accountant, give reasons that tie in to your service. If you are a baker, give reasons why your food is better.

30. Use a before-and-after-statement.

The Wrong Way and the Right Way to Buy a Used Car

This is a common way to show how your business can make a difference. If you own a gardening service, you might use a headline that suggests you transform gardens from jungles to parks. What you are doing here is comparing what people have (their problems) with what you can give them (the solution).

HOW TO TEST YOUR HEADLINE

Here is one way to find out if your headline will work—before you spend a cent to run it.

Ask yourself: "Can this headline be used for any competitor's ad, letter, or web site?" Imagine placing your headline on a competitor's copy. Will the headline still work? If so, change *yours*.

46

HYPNOTIC OPENINGS

These will easily help you start any writing almost without thinking. They are prompters, mind joggers, and brain stimuli. Just read them and fill in the blank with whatever comes to mind. For example, in your opening sentence tell your readers what they will learn or what feelings they will get from reading your words.

As you start reading the beginning of this article you find yourself . . .

As you sit there and read the beginning of this report you start to feel . . .

As you read every word of this report you will become (amazed, stunned, etc.) at . . .

As you analyze each word of this document, you will shortly feel a sense of (calmness, joy, etc.) . . .

As you scan every word of this web page you will begin to discover new ways of CREATING & DELIVERING VALUE

After you have read this short article, you will feel . . .

Can you imagine . .

Picture yourself five years from now . . .   AS YOU MIGHT WELL KNOW

Just picture . . .

Just imagine . . .

Remember when you were in high school . . .   PRODUCTIVITY INCREASE

Imagine what it would be like if . . .

Wouldn't it be amazing if . . .

And in those early years of existence . . .   HAS A DIRECT CORRELATION WITH PROFITABILITY INCREASE

AND GUIXT IS THE WORD EMBEDDED INTO AUTHORITY
YOUR SAP USER INTERFACE

Imagine what it would be like if you could . . .
See yourself . . .
Remember the smell of . . .
And you begin to notice . . .
Do you remember hearing . . .
Can you recall what a (insert word) feels like?

Tip: Use statements at the beginning of your writing that your prospects already know to be true. This creates trust right away. Trust leads to sales—and to getting people to do anything else you may want them to do. For example:

You probably know . . .
You're intelligent enough to know . . .
Of course you've heard that . . .
Everyone knows . . .
You probably already know this . . .
Rare thinking people like you already know that . . .

13 PSYCHOLOGICAL COPY CONNECTORS

"Copy connectors" are ways to weave your sentences and paragraphs together to end up with a web site that compels people to take the actions you want.

Tell your readers what they're thinking or feeling as they read your words. Most people will actually start thinking or feeling it because you brought it up. Only induce thoughts that will attract them to buy your product.

What if you . . .
Little by little you begin . . .
And as you absorb this information, you'll . . .
And as you are thinking about . . .
You become really interested . . .
Are you beginning to see how . . .
As you read each word in this letter, . . .
Have you noticed yet that . . .
Now I would like to help you experience . . .

[Handwritten margin notes:]

Fortunately for your shareholders you already own our enterprise software!

Like hidden nunchucks up the sleeve of your CEO (or you).

Imagine what it would be like if you could increase so much value that it will be unhidable

Wouldn't it be amazing if . . .
And you will sink deeper and deeper . . .
And you will start to feel better and better about . . .
The further and further you browse toward the end of this report,
  slowly your problem . . .

USING THE TIPS

As you can imagine, how you use those tips is up to you. But let me give you some pointers.

For example, you might have a line on your site that says, "My e-product gets results." You could rewrite that to say, "The further and further you read into this web site, the more you will realize that my e-product gets results."

See the difference?

The first line—"My e-product gets results"—is bland. The average web site contains that kind of limp writing.

The second line—"The further and further you read into this web site, the more you will realize that my e-product gets results"—is Hypnotic Writing. It conveys a command, and an assumption. Combined, they help lead to action.

Go through your web site—go through all your writing—with this in mind. Look for places to rewrite, add phrases, or in any other way grab and hold your visitor's attention. Remember: to create Hypnotic Writing, you have to focus on the interests of your visitors, not you.

Right?

47

HYPNOTIC QUIZ

Would you like to have a little fun right now? Here's a brief quiz to help you realize how easy it is to add the phrases and sentence starters from the preceding chapter to your writing: Go through this book—that's right, the one you are reading right now—and see if you can spot all the times I slipped in a hypnotic phrase.

Wouldn't it be amazing if you spotted every time I put a hypnotic twist on a sentence?

Clues:

"Wouldn't it be amazing if" is a phrase from the list in the preceding chapter.

You probably know that I've used Hypnotic Writing throughout these pages.

"You probably know" is also a phrase from the collection.

Are you beginning to see how easy this is?

"Are you beginning to see how" is also from the collection of phrases.

Now review this book and maybe highlight or underline all the places you spot Hypnotic Writing phrases.

Why not do it right now?

48

MY THREE BIGGEST SECRETS

Before I reveal my Hypnotic Writing formula, let me confess something few people know. The following secrets are the main reasons I'm able to write hypnotic copy. They'll probably surprise you. Brace yourself.

I DON'T DO THE WRITING

Shocked? What I mean is, I command or *request* the writing from my unconscious. This may startle you, but some of the greatest writers of all time did not *think* through their writing. Instead, they wrote it almost by dictation. In other words, they listened to something within and just wrote.

Ray Bradbury would write a story every day, never knowing what he would write until after he had written it.

Jack London disciplined himself to write 1,000 words every morning, whether he knew what to write or not.

Richard Webster, a friend and prolific author, writes 2,000 words every day—because he misheard the amount of words Jack London wrote.

Eugene Schwartz, the famous copywriter and author of *Breakthrough Advertising*, would set a timer and write in $33^1/_2$-minute spurts.

Eric Butterworth, a famous Unity minister and prolific author, would write what he called gibberish every morning, knowing that after he had started this spontaneous writing, it would soon take form and become his next radio sermon, weekly column, or book.

Dan Kennedy writes for one hour every morning, no matter what. He's one of the highest paid copywriters in the world.

What all of these writers are doing is keeping the door open to their unconscious. They are allowing creativity to visit them. They are letting the Muse know that they are available to receive new information.

I've learned to trust my unconscious. This is actually very hypnotic. Hypnotists know that our unconscious contains the answers to virtually all our questions, and has access to more than what we consciously know. This is why doing your home-work in the research phase is so critical. You are feeding your Muse, so to speak.

So my first big secret is that when I sit to write, I do it without much of an idea of what I will say. I have an *intention*, yes, but not a formulated plan. I'm doing that right now, as I type these words. I'm just typing as fast as I can, letting my unconscious direct what flows. I know I'll edit this later. As long as I know what is exciting, or unique, about the product or service I'm copywriting about, I'm fired up enough to start my draft.

That's my first secret.

I DIALOGUE IN MY MIND

My second secret may seem bizarre. What I do is imagine I am speaking to someone, telling them what I am writing, and I guess what their questions are. In short, I talk to myself—or at least talk to an imaginary reader in my mind.

In traditional selling, this is called paying attention to the objections and answering them. It's true in Hypnotic Writing as well. You want to cover all the bases, answer all the questions, give all the details, so your reader is well equipped to make a decision.

Dan Kennedy's tip is to think of all the reasons someone can possibly *not* buy your item. Whatever they might say, address it in some convincing way. For example:

> Not enough money? Offer a payment plan or send it with no payment required up front.
>
> No need for the item? List the various ways your prospect might use it.
>
> No belief in you? Offer testimonials, a guarantee, and anything else you can think of to prove your case.

I admit I'm doing a type of psychic mind reading act when I practice this second step, but I also confess that this is one of the biggest reasons my letters are so successful. I'm constantly rereading my letters, asking myself, "What is the reader asking here?" I then address it.

Far too much copy doesn't give enough information. I love buying stuff from catalogs and off the Internet. But when the catalog description doesn't answer all my questions, I don't buy. My friend Winston Marsh, Australia's famous marketing guru, says that when people are thinking about buying, they become information junkies. They want long copy. They want answers. My job is to anticipate their questions and answer them.

That's my second secret.

I PLUG IN HYPNOTIC LANGUAGE

This is where I shine. What I do is read my writing with my famous Swipe File at my side. I look for places to replace a phrase with a hypnotic statement.

You've already seen some of this at work earlier in this book. I often go through a letter a dozen times, reading it over, looking for places I can rewrite into a hypnotic statement. The Swipe File is my crutch and secret weapon here. I think anyone serious about writing persuasively needs to have the Swipe File. I'm not telling you that because I wrote the Swipe File (with Larry Dotson). I'm telling you that because it's the truth.

I can write about any product or service with the name of the product or service in my mind and the Swipe File in my hand. I won't be as hypnotic as I would be after doing research first, but the point is this: The Swipe File gives me power. Get it?

And that's my third secret.

49

HOW MUCH
IS THAT DOGGIE
IN THE WINDOW?

When I was in college, long, long ago, in another time and place, far, far away, I took care of a stray dog I later named Spot.

Yes, I really named her Spot. She was part beagle and part dalmatian, and she really had spots on her.

Well, my father would make fun of Spot, calling her a mutt. My father made fun of most of the things I was interested in, so this wasn't unusual behavior for him. Still, it irked me. I loved Spot. I thought she deserved better respect. So one day I made up a story:

> I told my dad that I had gone shopping at the grocery store, and of course had left Spot outside to wait for me. I then said that when I came out of the store, an old man was standing there, staring at Spot.
>
> "Is this your dog?" the man asked.
>
> "Yes," I replied, wondering what Spot had done while I was away.
>
> "You have a rare dog," he said.
>
> "I do?"

"Yes, this dog is a breed not seen much around here. This dog is probably worth a thousand dollars."

"Well, he's not for sale," I said, and left with Spot.

I told my father that simple story and from that moment on, he looked at Spot differently. He would play with Spot, feed Spot, and occasionally say nice things, such as, "That dog is pretty smart." Years later, when I had left college and my home, I left Spot with my family. My father took care of Spot until she died.

Now remember: The story I told my dad was fiction. It never happened. I told it to my father to do one thing and only one thing: *Change his perception.*

Before the story, Spot was a mutt. After the story, Spot was a collectible.

Perception is everything. I've often said that marketing is nothing but altering perceptions.

If that's true, how do you make it happen?

50

How to Change
Perception

Whenever you write your sales letter, you may need to change the reader's perception in order to get them to buy your product or service.

Don't think for a minute that I would encourage you to lie, cheat, steal, or in any other way mislead your reader. That's unethical and illegal. I lied to my father some 30 years ago because that's what my limited mental resources knew to do at that time. You don't need to lie to your customers. Not ever.

So how do you change the perceptions of your readers? You do it by putting things into perspective *before* you state them.

Say your product costs well over one thousand dollars. *Before* you tell prospects the price, prepare their mind for what you are about to say:

> You might point out that if they bought your product at a retail store, it would cost five thousand dollars.
>
> You might point out that if they had to create this product on their own, it might cost them 10 grand.
>
> You might point out that if they spent all the time and energy to create the product that you did to create it, it would have cost them thousands of dollars, months of work, and many sleepless nights.

In short, pave the way for your price by making it look small compared to something more expensive. Again, don't lie. Tell the truth. Think about what it would take for your reader to make or acquire or even do without your product. Describe all of that. *Then* tell your price.

This secret is known as *contrast.*

Scott Plous, in his book *The Psychology of Judgment and Decision Making* says, "For example, real estate agents sometimes exploit the contrast effect by showing buyers a run-down or overpriced property before they show the home that is under serious consideration."

At the risk of confusing you, let me bring in a little deeper psychology to prove my point. John Burton, in his heady book *States of Equilibrium* says people do not move toward success (pleasure) or away from failure (pain). He writes: "Rather, we move toward or away from the states of mind that we *associate* with success or failure."

What does that mean?

It means your reader has a mental concept about your offer, your price, and your product. All of those concepts are perceptions, not reality. They are mental associations based on how you described your product, price, and offer. You can influence and even change your reader's perceptions—their reality—by how you describe your product, price, and offer. You also influence how they will feel about your product, price, or offer by what you say *before* you ever describe them.

Again, when you paint a picture of life without your product, and then you paint a picture of life with your product, you've drawn a contrast and set up a perception. You can influence how your reader feels about your product this way.

My father mentally associated a mixed breed stray dog as a mutt. When I gave him a new view—that Spot was actually a *rare* breed worth lots of money—he altered his perception and ultimately his behavior. I sold him (so to speak) on Spot.

Remember, when you are writing, you have the power. You can influence how your reader perceives your message by how you describe it and what you compare it to.

This is Hypnotic Writing at full throttle.

THE MIND IS EASILY TRICKED

One of the secret principles you'll learn is the idea that the mind is easily tricked by optical as well as literary illusions.

You're probably familiar with optical illusions. Numerous books and sites show pictures that can be seen in a variety of ways. One famous image looks like an old woman—until you stare a little longer and suddenly see the profile of a young woman in the same image. (See Figure 49.1.)

Which do you see—an old woman or a young girl?

Both are there.

But maybe you've seen that famous illusion. Well, let me blow your mind. Look at Figure 49.2.

Figure 49.1   Optical Illusion—Old Woman or Young Girl?

Figure 49.2 Optical Illusion—Is It Moving?

Is the image moving?

Actually, it's not moving at all. Your mind is making you think it is. That's an optical illusion.

Something similar can happen with words. After all, words are images, too. They are subject to the blind spots in our brains. For proof, read the following:

Aoccdrnig to a rsceearcehr at Cmabrigde Uinervtisy, it deosn't mttaer in waht oredr the ltteers in a wrod are, the olny iprmoetnt tihng is taht the frist and lsat ltteer be at the rghit pclae. The rset can be a total mses and you can sitll raed it wouthit a porbelm. Tihs is bcuseae the huamn mnid deos not raed ervey lteter by istlef, but the wrod as a wlohe.

Fascinating, isn't it?

I'm *not* advocating misspelling words or intentionally misleading people. I'm demonstrating a principle. Your mind is vulnerable. It can see things that aren't there and miss things that are there. This is important information. It's what allows magicians the ability to fool us.

So how does this secret help you with your sales letters, ads, e-mails, web sites, and any other writing you do?

Here's how: You can consciously weave your words in such a way that people fill in the blanks. In other words, you can help them imagine buying your product or service without asking them to get it.

This is the sport of Hypnotic Writing. Here's an elementary example:

"Imagine driving this sleek car down a country road."

What did you see in your mind?

Most likely you imagined a sports car.

But why a *sports* car?

The word *sleek* led your mind to create a visual. That image came from your mind, not mine. I gave you a prompt and your mind leaped to a conclusion. Minds are like that.

Also, in the paragraph before that example, I planted the word *sport* in your mind. Did you notice it?

It's where I wrote, "This is the sport of Hypnotic Writing."

The word *sport* was already in your consciousness and was easy to bring up when I asked you to imagine a "sleek car."

I was talking with my friend Kevin Hogan, author of *The Psychology of Persuasion* and many other books about influence. He says that if you can actually get your customer to see themselves doing or using whatever your product does, you win big. The trick is, they have to imagine *themselves* with your product.

All of this may be tricky to grasp. Let's look at one more example:

I went to the MSN home page and saw a headline that read, *See a Ferrari Laptop.* I like sports cars, so I clicked. Imagine my surprise when I saw a picture of a laptop computer, not a convertible. My mind highlighted the word *Ferrari* and let me slide past the next word.

I could go on and on. For example, sometimes I end a letter with "Stop buy and see us." Few note I used the word *buy* instead of *by*. The mind sees it as "stop and buy."

I learned this subtle hypnotic method when a friend of mine out of town ended an e-mail with the words "Take car." He meant to say, "Take *care*." He slipped and wrote "Take car" as a way to speak to my mind and urge me to drive and see him.

In short, these "mind gaps" can be cause for confusion or for communication. The idea here is to use this principle to control how your reader pieces together your offer in your sales letter. What you tell them and how you tell it to them will create a picture in their mind, which creates their perception, which *is* their reality.

I remember an episode of *The Simpsons* where the unsophisticated bar owner, trying to seduce his date by offering to take her to dinner, said, "They have steaks there as big as toilet seats."

His description ruined the moment. Associating a steak with a toilet seat made the steak very unappealing.

When I was growing up, my father used to say he was proud of being bald. He would explain, "Grass doesn't grow on a busy street." His description created the impression—the perception— that bald people are thinkers.

But then one day someone told my dad, "You know, grass doesn't grow on concrete, either." This new description created a new perception.

Which is real? Both are.

When you are composing your Hypnotic Writing, be careful to lead your reader's mind where you want it to go. Again, how you describe your offer, price, or product will determine how they perceive it. And their perception *is* their reality.

Trevor Silvester, writing in his book *WordWeaving: The Science of Suggestion*, says: "We can never know reality."

Chew on *that* for a while.

51

At Last! The Joe Vitale Hypnotic Writing Formula

Now that you've learned an overview of some of the philosophy and psychology behind how I write copy that sells, let's get into my specific formula in a hands-on way. *This* is The Joe Vitale Hypnotic Writing Strategy. *This* is how I write copy. *This* is what can transform your copy from whatever it is right now to Hypnotic Writing.

Are you ready?

First, here are the five overall steps:

1. Intention: Directing Your Mind.
2. Research: Feeding Your Mind.
3. Creation: Unleashing Your Mind.
4. Rewrite: Sharpening Your Mind.
5. Test: Training Your Mind.

Now let's look at each step.

INTENTION

Intention means state your goal or desired outcome for your writing.

What do you want to achieve? Be specific. You don't want to write a sales letter. Anyone can do that. You want to write a sales letter that pulls in a certain number of orders. Whatever your intention, write it down. This programs your mind with a target.

When David Garfinkel, a terrific copywriter, was writing a challenging letter, he called me for some advice. I gave him one tip: "Ask yourself what it would take to get a 100% response."

Now, getting a 100% response from any copy would be a miracle, but it happens. Bruce Barton wrote a letter in 1925 that pulled a 100% response—everyone answered and everyone sent in money. (You can see the letter in my book *The Seven Lost Secrets of Success*.)

So what is your intention with the writing you are about to create? Go ahead and jot down your intention here.

_____

_____

_____

_____

While you're thinking about your intention, let me reveal a new way to direct your mind to help you create powerful Hypnotic Writing. I've never discussed this secret before. Ever. You're reading an exclusive news bulletin here.

Noah St. John is a dear friend, author of *Permission to Succeed*, and creator of a method he calls "Afformations." Now, affirmations are traditionally positive statements used to program your mind. "I am now wealthy," is an affirmation. "I now write hypnotic copy," is also an affirmation.

But Noah says those are limiting statements that don't engage the mind. Instead, he advises asking "why" questions. An example might be, "Why am I now wealthy?" Or "Why do I now write hypnotic copy?" He calls them *affor*mations.

Noah says the *why* questions awaken the mind and cause it to seek out answers to make the question's hidden statement come true. So when you ask, "Why am I now at my ideal weight?," you direct your mind to find the reasons and the method to achieve your ideal weight.

With all of this in mind, use a *why* question to help you create Hypnotic Writing. You might ask, "Why did my sales letter get a 100% response?" Or maybe, "Why am I now a wealthy hypnotic writer?"

You get the idea. Set an intention for your writing in any way that feels best for you. The idea is to direct your mind to achieve the results you desire.

Why not set an intention for your next piece of writing right now? You can build on what you wrote earlier, or try an "afformation" type of question. Write it here.

_____

_____

_____

_____

RESEARCH

Research means you have to do your homework.

I never write a letter for a product or a service until I've studied that product or service. You have to read all the literature, all previous marketing pieces, talk to customers, use the product, and so on.

When Tony Robbins' office wanted me to promote his new audio series called *The Edge*, I asked to see it. Even though Robbins is world famous and known for his high-quality material, I needed to see the material to absorb all I could about it.

You never know where you'll get an insight. David Ogilvy found the headline for one of his famous ads by reading the technical manuals for the car he was advertising. The headline is now legendary: "At 60 miles an hour the loudest noise in this new Rolls-Royce comes from the electric clock."

Dan Kennedy once told me a copywriter's job is to pull out of the company owner what he can't or won't say. Talk to the people who sell the product. Talk to the owner. In conversation, they may say something you can use in your copy.

This is the "feeding your brain" part of copywriting. Soak up all the facts before you can write a word of copy. Otherwise, you're writing fiction.

My own little secret is that I look at a product or service for what is exciting about it. Since excitement is contagious and excitement sells, I assume that once I find the excitement in a product or service, I can then radiate my own feelings of excitement, through my words, out to my readers. Those readers then turn into buyers.

Another secret is that I try to come up with a working headline based on my research. The headline acts as a "thought handle" for me. It anchors the basic message of the letter *for me*. I may change the headline later. For now, it serves as a focal point for my mind.

Robert Collier, author of *The Robert Collier Letter Book* (the greatest manual on writing letters ever written by anyone, ever), said people want news. What I do is think like a reporter. I review the literature for whatever I want to sell, and I look for what is new about it. Is the product new? Is there a new use for it? How will this product be new to my readers? News will grab and hold attention, so I eagerly look for it in my research.

Spend a few minutes here jotting down some points, some facts, based on your research about the item you want to sell.

_____

_____

_____

_____

_____

_____

_____

_____

_____

_____

_____

_____

_____

_____

CREATION

Creation means production.

I tend to create rough first drafts at lighting speed. This is the step where you create your first draft. Not your *final* draft but your *first* draft. My secret is to turn off the editorial part of my mind so my creative side has free license.

In my software program, Hypnotic Writing Wizard, we include a function called Unconscious Directed Writing. It's a way to turn off your inner editor. Choose that function in the software and the screen goes blank. Then type, without stopping, for whatever specified time you set. When you've finished, click Escape and the screen comes back and your writing was saved.

The idea is to disconnect the editor from the writer. You need both functions, but not at the same time. This is a major secret to writing hypnotically. The more you can ignore—for the time being—that voice in your head trying to rewrite your words as you write them, the greater the odds of your producing a quality first draft.

Again, the secret to this step is to write spontaneously. The basic rule is: *Do not stop writing!* Later, in the next step, you can do all the editorial revisions you want. For now, just write.

Write a first draft for your sales letter here.

_____

_____

_____

_____

_____

_____

_____

_____

_____

_____

_____

_____

_____

_____

_____

_____

_____

_____

_____

_____

_____

_____

_____

REWRITE

Rewrite means there are no great writers, there are only great rewriters.

While I urge you to write your first draft as fast as humanly possible, without checking to correct anything or look up anything, I also urge you to review your work, later, in this rewriting stage.

This is where you polish your gem. This is where you change passive words to active words, lame sentences to hypnotic ones. Rewriting is where you become a word sculptor and redesign your copy, moving words, sentences, even entire paragraphs.

There are secrets to doing this, of course. Here are a few of my favorites:

- Use Stephen King's advice. Make 10 copies of your sales letter. Hand them to 10 peers (not family members). When their feedback comes in, look for the majority votes.
- Whenever you see a comma, see if you can change it to a period. People often write sentences way too long. Rather than using commas to set off clauses in a sentence, try using a period and creating several shorter sentences. This will make your writing "move."
- Write in active language. Passive language is boring. Active language is hypnotic. This is a major secret, even though it's been written about by everyone from E.B. White in the famous 1918 book *The Elements of Style* to me. For example: "The book was read by me" is passive, while "I read the book" is active. Here's a tip: Look for the helping words *were, is, was, are,* or *be* as a way of spotting passive sentences.
- Pretend someone will pay you $1,000 for every word you take out of your letter. Edit ruthlessly.
- Rearrange paragraphs. Most great writers are word sculptors. They move paragraphs around like chess pieces on a game board. Pretend you are the Michelangelo of words. Rearrange your writing to make the most sense.
- Have a dialogue with your reader. This is one my greatest secrets. I practice my psychic skills when I write copy. I am always

wondering, "What will be on my reader's mind at this point in the letter?" I then address their question at that point.

- Insert hypnotic commands. This is also one of my biggest secrets. I go through my draft and add, change, or rewrite current statements into truly hypnotic ones. This is where I rely on such tools as the Hypnotic Writer's Swipe File, which I absolutely love.

- Read your writing out loud. This can be very revealing. When you speak your words, you are forced to slow down and become more aware of them. But here's an even bigger secret: Get someone to read your writing to you. This can make any errors, awkward sentences, or anything else glaringly obvious. If the person reading your writing stumbles, wrinkles their brow, or seems confused, take note of where they are in your writing *and fix it.*

- Ask yourself, "Where will someone probably skip a section in my writing?" Trust your intuition. If you sense a paragraph may be boring, rewrite it, break it into smaller sections, or delete it. As a famous novelist once said, "I try to leave out the parts people skip." Here's a secret to remember: There are three kinds of readers: *Word-for-word* readers, *skimmers*, and *jumpers*. Skimmers scan your writing looking for key words, benefits, subheadlines, and so on. Jumpers do the same thing, but faster, jumping from headline to subhead to offer to P.S., looking for your main message. Your writing has to appeal to all three kinds of readers. Keep them in mind as you rewrite.

- Use the checklist (you'll read about it in the next chapter) to review your writing, looking at specific key areas for possible improvement.

Go through the letter you wrote earlier and see if you can use these tips to rewrite it. For now, just experiment. Do that here:

_____

_____

TESTING

Testing means you aren't smart enough to know what people want.

You can't guess. Write your best copy, rewrite it, and then give it to the market to see if it causes them to buy.

Testing is the great god of marketing. Without it, you're shooting at a flying pigeon in a dark room. Good luck in hitting anything but the wall or the ceiling.

The Internet makes testing easy. Just e-mail your letter to your list, put up your web site, or run a Google ad. The idea is to see how your letter does in the marketplace.

Jot down some ways you can test your copy before you send it out.

_____

_____

_____

_____

_____

_____

_____

_____

_____

_____

_____

_____

_____

There you have it. That process is what I go through to write Hypnotic Copy. The more you do it, the better you'll get at it.

52

A NEW HYPNOTIC
COPY CHECKLIST

The following list is my own secret checklist. After you have written your first draft and polished it, use the following list to check your writing's potency.

Note: You'll see a new question, the last one, about graphics. I think graphics are not used wisely enough in copy, off-line or not. Graphics can help get attention, demonstrate your product, and reinforce your selling message.

- Does your opening pull readers into the ad with fast, compelling, strong reader interest? Does the opening begin with a *bang*?
- Does the copy move along at a swift, easy-to-read clip, generating desire all the way? Is it boring?
- Is the copy written in the conversational style of the person who is going to read it? Have you spoken on the same wavelength as your readers?
- Is the copy visually attractive and inviting, using short sentences, short words, short paragraphs, bullets, subheads, and other visual aids?
- Does the copy overcome objections and answer all questions? Is the ad a complete selling argument?

- Does the copy include proof and create believability with testimonials, specific details, and a guarantee? Can your prospects read this and remain skeptical?
- Does the copy end with a powerful call to action—a request to fill out a form, call, or visit your business? Do you tell readers what to do?
- Is the copy written from the viewpoint of what the readers will get? Do readers know how their lives will be improved?
- Is it clear what you are selling? Is there one central offer?
- Does the copy reveal what is new, unique, or different about your small business? Can your competitors also use this copy?
- Is there a deadline or some other logical reason for a reader to act *now*? Can your prospects read this and put the ad aside to respond later?
- Are there plenty of reasons to buy? Since people want to buy, have you convinced them *why* they should?
- Does your copy follow and complete what your headline begins?
- Have you reminded your readers of what happens if they do not buy?
- Have you tightened the copy so you say what you have to say in the fewest words possible? Have you let others edit the copy for you?
- Is this the best you can do? (Are you being honest?)
- Have you included a graphic that gets attention? Is it appropriate? Does it demonstrate the product or service? Does it reinforce your message?

53

THE FIVE SECRET
LAWS OF HYPNOTIC
PERSUASION

I've never revealed these five secret laws before. They will help you create truly riveting Hypnotic Writing.

Here they are.

1. *Engagement.* The more you can engage your reader, the more inclined they'll be to buy your item when you ask for the order. Ask questions. Ask them to complete a task. Make your site interactive. Do you know what I mean? ☺

2. *Choice.* Give people a choice that are win-wins for both you and him or her. One item offered to buy or not buy is not a good choice. Two items to buy—to choose between—gives the reader a sense of control. "Do you want this now or later?" implies they *will* want it.

3. *Ego.* Stroke their ego, but sincerely. Don't lie. Don't mislead. We all want flattery. You. Me. All of us. Pet a dog and he'll follow you home. You're smart, so you already know this. ☺

4. *Reward.* Reward people who do what you ask—such as buy from you. Give them bonuses, premiums, unexpected extras. This creates value, removes buyer's remorse, and strokes the ego.

5. *Curiosity*. What's the most powerful psychological tool any Hypnotic Writer can use? I use this one every day. I might make a call to a friend and say, "Guess how much the most expensive Mercedes-Benz in history just sold for?" I won't tell them until I'm done saying whatever I called to say. My question opens their mind—engages them, yes—but also locks them onto my every word. At the end, I'll tell them a 1929 two-seater Mercedes-Benz just sold for over four million dollars, thereby completing the story. (A true story, too.)

See how many places you can use these secret laws in your writing. Make some notes here.

_____

_____

_____

_____

_____

54

THE SEVEN MOST HYPNOTIC BOOKS OF ALL TIME

J ay Abraham, famous marketing strategist, interviewed me, Dan Kennedy, and Jay Conrad Levinson one night. Jay asked each of us what our two favorite books were. I took a breath. Jay heard it.

"Books are your life, aren't they?" Jay asked me, knowing I'm a bookaholic with a giant collection of treasured works.

I found it hard to reply then, just as I find it hard to narrow the list down to a handful of books that I think are the most hypnotic of all time, at least for the purposes of learning how to write hypnotically. Nevertheless, I've done it. The list follows.

If you are serious about becoming a powerful Hypnotic Writer, then you need to study these books—at least these—as if they were handed to you by a superpower, a god, or the source of life itself. These books changed my life. Whatever it takes for you to get them, *get them.*

The Robert Collier Letter Book by Robert Collier. I was an average writer before reading this book. I was a Hypnotic Writer after it. More professional copywriters say this book changed their writing talents for the better more than any other book. You can get this masterpiece, in hardcover or paperback, from Collier's family. See http://www.RobertCollierPublications.com.

The Art of Readable Writing by Rudolf Flesch. This book opened my eyes. Flesch taught a simple method of communicating. Basically, write as you speak. He also invented the famous Readability Formula, which is a way to test how hard, or easy, your writing is to read. While this original book is now out of print, a wonderful new edition is available with the title *The Classic Guide to Better Writing: Step-by-Step Techniques and Exercises to Write Simply, Clearly and Correctly.* Amazon and bookstores sell it.

Unlimited Selling Power: How to Master Hypnotic Selling Skills by Donald Moine and Kenneth Lloyd. This is the book that triggered my idea to write *Hypnotic Writing*, way back in 1990. This excellent work explains *conversational hypnosis*, which is very close to Hypnotic Writing in style and technique. Amazon and bookstores sell it.

How to Write a Good Advertisement: A Short Course in Copywriting by Victor Schwab. This 1962 gem is still valid today, no matter what you are writing. This basic course taught me the key elements of how to sell with words. It's still in print, usually available from Amazon, bookstores, or from http://www.MPowers.com.

Million Dollar Mailings by Denison Hatch. A beautiful hardcover book revealing the inside story on 71 successful direct mail letters. A terrific way to become a great writer is to study great writings. Get this one and lock yourself in a room with it. Also get Hatch's other book, *Method Marketing*, which reveals how to get inside the heads of your readers. Brilliant stuff. At Amazon or from bookstores.

Covert Hypnosis by Kevin Hogan. Get this little known resource to understand hypnotic language patterns and much more, from body language to unconscious influence, all by a well-known and highly respected persuasion expert. Only available from http://www.KevinHogan.com.

How to Write Letters that Sell: Winning Techniques for Achieving Sales through Direct Mail by Christian Godefroy and Dominique Glocheux. I love this book. It breaks down the process of how to write persuasive letters so anyone can do it. The examples are worth gold. The 21-point checklist is priceless. The only bad news is this book is now out of print. You might search eBay, Amazon, or www.abebooks.com for a used copy. It's worth the hunt.

OTHER BOOKS TO READ

Anything by John Caples.
Anything by Dan Kennedy.
Anything by Bob Bly.
Anything by Joe Sugarman.
Anything by David Garfinkel.
Anything by Joe Vitale. ☺

MORE RESOURCES

The Power of Outrageous Marketing by Joe Vitale. The Nightingale-Conant bestselling audio package includes books, workbook, and more. See http://www.nightingale.com to hear audio excerpts online and/or to order.

Power Persuasion is a terrific course on NLP and persuasion by hypnotist David Barron. See http://www.changework.com/adcopy/persuasion.htm. I love his course and have bought multiple copies of it to give to students, clients, and friends.

How to Think like Joe Vitale is an online audio program where NLP expert Tellman Knudsen figured out what makes me tick as a copywriter. Fascinating stuff, if I do say so myself. See http://www.nlp-expert.com/thinklikejoevitale.html

Hypnotic Writing Wizard my Windows-based software program designed to help you write sales letters, ads, news releases, speeches, and even entire books using Hypnotic Writing methods. Get all the details at http://www.HypnoticWriting Wizard.com.

55

THE HYPNOTIC
WRITING FORMULA

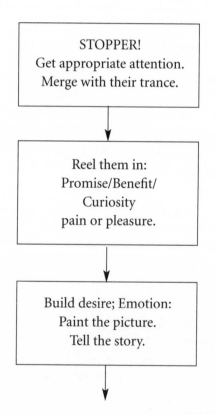

STOPPER!
Get appropriate attention.
Merge with their trance.

Reel them in:
Promise/Benefit/
Curiosity
pain or pleasure.

Build desire; Emotion:
Paint the picture.
Tell the story.

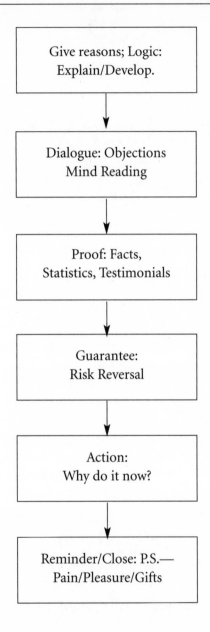

56

YOUR CHALLENGE

A few years ago marketing guru and friend John Reese broke all previous sales records and made over $1,000,000 in 24 hours online.

His true story is inspiring and instructive. You can read an entire report detailing his incredible success at http://www.mrfire.com /trafficspecial.zip. And if you haven't seen his product yet, see http://www.trafficsecrets.com/jvitale.

My point in bringing John into the picture is this: miracles happen all the time. Records are broken. The bar gets lifted. And the adventure continues. Who knows what record will be broken next—and by whom? After John's success, several others went after huge sales in one day online, including me. You may be next.

Your Hypnotic Writing skills can do magical, miraculous, and maybe even impossible things. I once wrote a sales letter that pulled a 91% response. Bruce Barton once wrote a fundraising letter that nailed a 100% response. (Both letters are in my book *The Seven Lost Secrets of Success.*

The potential for you to do better than I, Barton, or even John Reese is there.

I've given you the tools. You have the hammer, the nails, and the ruler.

Now the question is this: What are you going to build? The choice is yours.

Do good things.

Appendix

HYPNOTIC E-MAILS

I've managed to create a following online, all through e-mail. I have a large mailing list of responsive buyers who have made me wealthy. They've made my books bestsellers. I'm told my list will out-pull lists a hundred times larger. How? What's the secret to making my e-mails profitable? I think there are five secrets.

Let's analyze some e-mails I've written and see if we can find the secrets.

Ready?

Subject: Can you answer these questions?

Can you answer these questions?

- How do you keep a steady stream of copywriting concepts flowing from your brain to your fingertips?
- What beliefs are necessary to write compelling copy?
- How do you choose projects that will motivate you from start to finish?
- What are the key techniques for creating a rock-solid successful mind-set?
- What three words can you say to yourself to unlock a literal flood of ideas?

- What single technique will literally allow you to look at your business through the eyes of Joe Vitale?
- How can you notice a gold mine of hidden opportunities by changing one single thing about how you focus?
- What can you change about how you grew up to amplify your creativity?
- What happens to your success mind-set when you use NLP to change your past?
- How can you set your brain up to develop copywriting motivation instantly?
- How can you instantly eliminate fear of success?
- What can you do to rapidly turn each of your previous failures into amazing opportunities?
- How can you develop a successful mind-set by learning to use the parts of you that are holding you back?

If you want to know the answers to these questions, see http://www.nlp-expert.com/thinklikejoevitale.html.

Go for it.

Dr. Joe Vitale
President, Hypnotic Marketing, Inc.

Subject: 60 average people sell ordinary products online and *win.*

Sorry to interrupt your weekend but—I just came across a new e-book that reveals the success stories of 60 average people—not marketing people or salespeople or geniuses but average people—who are now making incredible money selling ordinary products online. Talk about inspiring. Talk about showing the road-map to success. You can get all the details at http://www.profitautomation.com/app/aftrack.asp?afid=144712.

All 60 people are outside the Internet marketing community, and all are thriving online.

These people include:

- A guy making $950,000 a year selling *socks*.
- A guy making millions on eBay selling other people's stuff on consignment.
- A guy who generated $1.2 million last year selling magic tricks.
- A college professor who earns over $100,000 a year selling juggling supplies.
- A lady who earned $450,000 last year selling jokes and party items.

My friend John interviewed these people and asked some very probing questions. What amazes me is that they answered them. They basically laid all aspects of their online business out there for the world to see. They give:

- Their URLs.
- How long it took them to get profitable.
- How much time they invest in their businesses.
- What products and services they offer.
- How they deal with suppliers.
- How they deliver the product.
- Current and projected revenues.
- Web site statistics.
- How they designed their sites and how they drive traffic to them.
- Their proven Internet marketing model.
- Any offline marketing they do.
- How they handle customer service.
- Tools and resources they use.
- Advice they offer other entrepreneurs.

The interviews in this book are nothing short of amazing. They are so full of ideas and information on exactly how they are doing it that I'm actually in the process of reading the book twice. See http://www.profitautomation.com/app/aftrack.asp?afid=144712.

I just had to take a break in the middle of my second reading and share this book with you. It contains all of the information that I found myself wishing I could pass on to you all this time. This book literally is an answer to a prayer.

Now I feel that I can finally share with you how you can build a thriving business in your own niche. You can build a business around products or services that ordinary, everyday people are interested in.

Take a look at it, and see if it doesn't completely blow you away, too. This is the very first time that you've read about this book, because it's brand new. John just finished the interviews and editing the book.

Grab a copy, and devote part of the weekend to devouring it. If you're like me, you won't be able to put it down once you start, though. It's 281 pages, so don't say I didn't warn you.

And I didn't even mention the guy making $18 million per year, selling something *very* ordinary over the Internet.

Now the only question is: "Do you really want a successful online business that will provide you with the lifestyle you and your family deserve?"

If so, head over to http://www.profitautomation.com/app/aftrack.asp?afid=144712.

Go for it.

Dr. Joe Vitale
President, Hypnotic Marketing, Inc.
#1 Best-Selling Author *Spiritual Marketing*.
Author of way too many other books to list here.
See http://www.MrFire.com.

Subject: Need money? A teleseminar on grants

How much money do you need?

Grants may be the way to raise the funds you need for your business, project, or even for real estate.

Don't dismiss this by thinking you know how, why, or if you can get a grant for your needs. Instead, tune in to this teleseminar (it's free) this Tuesday, June 1, at 7 P.M. Central (8 Eastern, 5 Pacific) and get the facts from a veteran grant finder.

Call (507) 726-3200 and enter 44455#.

You'll then hear me (Joe Vitale) spend one hour interviewing grants expert Jillian Coleman about the inside secrets of getting grants today. You'll find this lively, informative, inspiring, surprising, and even freee. (You just pay for the phone call.)

Come early, as we only have 250 lines open. (We'll record the call for later access, though.)

And if you can't wait till Tuesday, keep reading.

Power Your Business with Free Money is a nine-week e-course on finding grants and writing powerful grant proposals. It's the equivalent of a graduate degree in grant writing, delivered to you via e-mail. Best of all, it entitles you to Jillian's personal mentoring and guidance. Let her help you develop your project, find funding, and produce your own grant proposal. Also included: great bonuses. Check it out at http://www.grantmerich.com/1pybJV.htm.

Jillian's newest class is Create Your Own Non-Profit, a three-week e-mail course that teaches you everything you need to know to set up a nonprofit corporation. Learn how to structure a Board of Directors, how to get tax-exempt status from the IRS, how to start raising money, and much more. This course also includes Jillian's one-on-one assistance with your project, some wonderful bonuses, and that special price. Find out more at http://www.grantmerich.com/1cyonpJV.htm.

And if you'd like to sign up for both classes, you can take advantage of an even deeper discount. Jillian is taking $300 extra off the combined price, when you enroll in both Power Your Business with Freee Money, and Create Your Own Non-Profit. If you'd like the special deal for both classes, just e-mail Jillian directly; she's always happy to answer questions. Reach her at: jillian@GrantMeRich.com.

Remember, the free teleseminar with me interviewing Jill is *this* Tuesday (June 1st) at 7 P.M. Central (8 Eastern, 5 Pacific). Call (507) 726-3200 and enter 44455#.

Call early and say hi, then listen as Jill reveals some information you can literally take to the bank.

Mark your calendar and pass the word.

Thank you.

Joe Vitale
President, Hypnotic Marketing, Inc.
#1 Best-Selling Author *Spiritual Marketing*.
Author of way too many other books to list here.
See http://www.MrFire.com.

Hypnotic Marketing, Inc.
121 Canyon Gap Rd.
Wimberley TX 78676-6314

Member BBB Online 2004

Subject: How to feel good about money

Eva Gregory wants me *bad*.

How do I know? She just sent me a private e-mail inviting me to grab a copy of her hot new book, *The Feel Good Guide to Prosperity* for a dramatic 30% discount.

Oh, yeah. She wants me. Her book isn't even in stores yet and here she is, dangling a discount to get me interested in it/her.

Wait a minute.

I just re-read her e-mail to me. She says *anyone* can have that discount, as long as they order her printed book at the prepublication price before July 13, 2005. See http://www.leadingedgecoaching.com/feelgoodguide.html.

Get this: Not only did Eva get me to promote her book to you, but I'm not getting a dime for doing this.

My lucky day.

Actually, it's *your* lucky day.

Her book is terrific. See complete details at http://www
.leadingedgecoaching.com/feelgoodguide.html.

I still think Eva wants me, but for now we'll just have to read
each other's books.

Sorry, Eva.

Joe Vitale
President, Hypnotic Marketing, Inc.
#1 Best-Selling Author *Spiritual Marketing*.

Subject: Britney Spears Caught Using Hypnotic Selling in TV
Ad

FOR IMMEDIATE RELEASE
Phone: (512) 847-3414
E-mail: News@mrfire.com

> Britney Spears Caught Using
> Hypnotic Selling in TV Ad
> Unless Curiosity stinks,
> sales will not, says expert

Austin, TX—The pop singer sex kitten Britney Spears may be
using forbidden "Hypnotic Selling" methods in her TV commercial promoting her new fragrance, "Curious," claims
marketing expert Dr. Joe Vitale of http://www.Hypnotic
WritingWebcast.com.

"Her ad plays on sexuality, mystery, and curiosity," ex-
plains Vitale, a specialist on hypnotic persuasion methods.
"Even the name invokes the most powerful motivator of all:
Curiosity."

Spears announced her new product at Macy's in New York
City on September 14. She's being paid an estimated $12
million to promote the Elizabeth Arden product.

"Unless her perfume truly stinks, people are going to buy it almost mindlessly," says Vitale, who is giving a webcast on October 5, 2004, to alert people to how hypnotic persuasion methods work. See http://www.HypnoticWritingWebcast.com.

Vitale says the TV commercial featuring Spears begins with images that seem to be a soap opera, but then quickly become a sexual fantasy come to life. The ad almost dares you to buy the perfume, he adds.

"Even her music has elements of hypnosis in it," states Vitale, a certified hypnotherapist as well as author of such books as *Hypnotic Writing*.

For more information see http://www.HypnoticWriting Webcast.com.

Subject: A big fat confession from Dr. Joe Vitale

If you've been reading my newsletters, you know I've lost almost 60 pounds in the past six months.

I've done it primarily with the help of the most remarkable training I've ever seen.

I'm talking about The Mental Toughness Institute.

The people there have helped me to raise my consciousness, expose delusional thinking,

and finally—finally!—reach my fitness goals.

Whether you have 10 pounds or 100 pounds to lose, this program can help you, too.

I've gone through their 12-week program twice, and I will enter it a third and final time in a couple of weeks.

Why three times?

It's simply my choice. You can take the course once and get what you need. I lost 40 pounds in the first 12 weeks.

Because I love the program and want additional support as I pursue my fitness goals, I am entering the program again.

I'm writing to invite you to join me in one of their two next classes.

The training is done with CDs (which are brilliant), reading (which is eye-opening), homework (which takes a few minutes daily), and coaching-by-phone (which is priceless).

It's a very psychological as well as spiritual approach. And it influences every area of your life. You learn how to think like a world-class champion. Even my income went up as I did the trainings.

Believe me, when I first heard about their program, I was skeptical. But I was sick and tired of being overweight, and I had decided I was doing something about it once and for all. And since the price for the training is so low, I just took the jump.

And I am forever grateful I did.

I'm a new man.

The training is conducted by the same people who published the book I think is a masterpiece (which they just recorded on 12 CDs) called, *177 Mental Toughness Secrets of the World Class.*

Again, I invite you to take the next training with me. This program can help you get to where you want to be. It worked for me, and I had struggled with obesity for almost 50 years. Obviously, it can work for you, too.

It's all explained at http://www.mentaltoughnessinstitute.com.

The folks at the institute were not going to do another training for a long time, as they are also busy speakers, but I persuaded them to offer another class because *I* wanted in it again. They agreed, as long as I agreed to tell some people about it. That's what I'm doing with this note to you.

Seating is limited, and I already have the first spot.

The new training dates are Mondays at noon Eastern beginning February 21, 2003 (that's the one I'll be in), and Thursday nights at 9:00 P.M. Eastern beginning February 24.

Choose one of them.

And you, too, can finally achieve the body you dream of.

Want proof?

See recent pictures of me at the bottom of http://www.mr fire.com/photogallery.html.

Then sign up at http://www.mentaltoughnessinstitute.com.

See you on the calls.

Go for it.

Dr. Joe Vitale
*Aude aliquid dignum**
President, Hypnotic Marketing, Inc.
Creator of www.hypnoticsellingformula.com.
Author of way too many books to mention here.
See www.MrFire.com or www.Amazon.com.

*Sixteenth-century Latin: "Dare something worthy."

Subject: Who's the best copywriter around? (No, not me, but thanks.)

There are only a handful of copywriters around today whom I respect. One of them just came out with a home study course.

Even though I'm a full-time copywriter with dozens of books and even my own course out there, I signed up for this man's new system.

So if you are interested in earning $150,000+ a year writing copy underneath a coconut tree, then keep reading.

When it comes to writing compelling marketing copy that grabs the prospect's attention and propels them into buying, Randy Gage is the real deal. I love his style.

This man is a copywriting genius. He has made millions of dollars for himself and his clients writing copy from a sidewalk cafe in Paris, under a palm tree in Hawaii, and from the comforts of his own home.

And now he is willing to share his secrets and techniques so you, too, can become a world-class copywriter in his amazing new resource.

Randy Gage's One-Year Copywriting Home Study Course

How to Write Killer Copy for Sensational Sales of any Product or Service Even If *You* Flunked English.

You see, copy is the backbone of all great marketing campaigns. You can make a fortune writing sales letters, brochures, ads, and web sites for businesses.

There are simply millions of companies looking to hire great copywriters. Of course, you may not want to be looking to hire yourself out as a copywriter. You may want to use the skills you will learn in this resource for building your own business.

By the time you are done with this one-year course, you will be able to:

- Create money-producing web sites.
- Write a best-selling book.
- Create compelling sales letters, brochures, catalogs, and other marketing materials.
- Design ads that pull in orders like crazy.
- Create a product catalog that brings in tens of thousands of dollars a month.

When you have finished this home study course, you will be able to write powerful, gut-wrenching, killer copy that moves people to take action. Get all the details at http://www.TheCopywritingcourse.com.

And remember, I signed up for this course, too.

Randy is the real deal, and I only want to learn from the best. You can, too.

Go for it.

Dr. Joe Vitale
President, Hypnotic Marketing, Inc.
Creator of www.hypnoticsellingformula.com.
Author of way too many books to mention here.
See www.MrFire.com or www.Amazon.com.

Hypnotic Marketing, Inc.
121 Canyon Gap Rd.
Wimberley, TX 78676

Member BBB Online 2005

Subject: A private invitation to join my Executive Mentoring Program

How much better would you do in your business if you were personally trained by an already successful person?

For the next five days I will be accepting applications for my brand new Executive Mentoring Program.

This is an exclusive, one-on-one opportunity to work with me and the marketing professionals I've trained. We will reveal my proven marketing secrets and strategies that have turned ordinary people into millionaires.

If you think you may be interested, please see this site, which explains the program and contains an application. It's at http://www.joe-vitale-executive-mentoring.com/info.html.

Obviously, I can't accept everyone. If you're at all interested in doing better in your business, please visit the link now and complete the application.

I look forward to hearing from you.

Go for it.

Dr. Joe Vitale
Aude aliquid dignum*
President, Hypnotic Marketing, Inc.
Creator of www.hypnoticsellingformula.com.

Author of way too many books to mention here.
See www.MrFire.com or www.Amazon.com.

Hypnotic Marketing, Inc.
121 Canyon Gap Rd.
Wimberley, TX 78676

Member BBB Online 2005

*Sixteenth-century Latin: "Dare something worthy."

Subject: Today's the day I chase Harry Potter up a tree

It's April 5—finally.

Today I plan to chase Harry Potter up a tree.

And you can help me do it.

Get one or more copies of my latest book, *The Attractor Factor: 5 Easy Steps for Creating Wealth (or anything else) From the Inside Out* today, and you can have over 23 bonuses— some worth thousands of dollars—and you could even win a Caribbean cruise for two.

See http://www.mrfire.com/factor for details.

Some of the bonuses not described on that page include:

- The Relationship Attractor Factor.
- Envisioneering—Creating a Master Life Vision.
- 20 Tips for Husbands and Wives to Enhance and Save Their Marriage.
- The Enlightened Salesperson: Selling from the Inside Out.
- How to Make Someone Feel like a Million Bucks.
- What Every Woman Needs to Know about Weight and Stress.
- The Complete Guide to Internet Marketing.
- 101 Best Tools and Resources to Running Your Internet Business.
- Meet and Grow Rich: How to Create a Master Mind Group.
- Secret National Television Media Lists by a publicist.

The list goes on, of course.

There are over 23 bonuses.

They are worth thousands.

You'll also get access to my recent interview of Joe Sugarman, the genius behind Blueblocker sunglasses, called "How to Create an Empire with a $50 Product." It alone is worth gold. (It's never been heard before.)

And there are some surprise bonuses, too. One of them is a recent audio where Dan Kennedy interviewed—well, you'll have to discover that one when you get all the bonuses.

All you have to do is get my new book, *The Attractor Factor: 5 Easy Steps for Creating Wealth (or anything else) from the Inside Out* today.

This is the book one reviewer said "could change humanity."

There is some surprising and even shocking material in my new book, which is the revised, expanded, and three times better version of my bestselling *Spiritual Marketing* book, including:

- What's Your Prosperity IQ?
- How to Attract Money.
- A Shortcut to Attracting Whatever You Want.
- The Shocking True Story of Jonathan.
- The Experiment.

There's also a beautiful introduction by Dr. Robert Anthony.

And that's all on top of discovering the five-step formula that will help you attract what you really want.

The book reveals, once and for all, the missing secret to success, manifestation, and happiness.

Again, see http://www.mrfire.com/factor.

Just be sure to do this before midnight tonight. When you do, we can give Harry Potter a run for his money and my new book might reach enough people to actually awaken the planet.

It's worth a shot, isn't it?

Be sure to tell your friends, too. Forward this e-mail to anyone you care about.

Let's make a difference.

Go for it.

Dr. Joe Vitale
President, Hypnotic Marketing, Inc.
Creator, www.HypnoticMarketingStrategy.com.
Author of way too many books to mention here.
See www.MrFire.com or www.Amazon.com.

Hypnotic Marketing, Inc.
121 Canyon Gap Rd.
Wimberley, TX 78676

Member BBB Online 2005

Subject: About your brain

My basic philosophy in life is
"Anything is possible."

I may not know how to achieve something, but I certainly know there is a way to achieve anything I can imagine. I just have to find, or sometimes create, that way.

"Anything is possible" is my current chant—the slogan that carries me through every day.

It's helped me achieve some impressive results, from best-selling books to an 80-pound weight loss.

Where did I get this idea?

Why am I so optimistic about life, anyway?

Glad you asked.

Truth is, I'm a student of Pelmanism.

Pelman what?

Pelman-ism.

Most people are pessimists.

You know who they are.

If you won the lotto, and were suddenly so rich you were ready to shop for a castle to live in, they'd be the ones asking, "But what about the taxes?"

Well, I'm tired of pessimists.

Life is how you look at it. Look for the doom and gloom, and you'll find it. Plenty of people out there willing to tell you how bad the world is.

But look for the sunshine and gold, and you'll find that, too. It's just a matter of where you point your mental binoculars.

It all comes down to how you use your main muscle—the one few people ever flex.

I'm talking about your brain.

Most people have no control over their brain.

To prove it, go ahead and stop your thoughts.

I'll wait while you quit thinking.

(Really try to stop your thoughts—or even just the negative ones—the ones asking you why you're reading this—yeah, those thoughts—go ahead—stop them.)

Couldn't do it, could you?

You're not alone. Few can. We simply haven't been trained to take our brains and make them do what we want. Instead, our brains chase us around all day.

Pat O'Bryan and I just breathed life into a long lost course that shows you how to make your main muscle work for you. It's called Pelmanism. It's described at http://www.pelmanism online.com.

If you're ready to join the club of high achievers that Pat and I belong to, go see that site.

Won't cost you a nickel to go look.

And there's a pretty riveting introduction there by me on How to Find Your Super Powers.

You'll also learn all about the Pelmanism course.

And you won't find a pessimist anywhere on the page: http://www.pelmanismonline.com.

See you there (unless you let your mind talk you out of it).

Go for it.

Dr. Joe Vitale
President, Hypnotic Marketing, Inc.
Author of way too many books to mention here, except the #1 bestseller, *The Attractor Factor.*

P.S. Have you seen the new and improved www.MrFire.com?

Hypnotic Marketing Inc
121 Canyon Gap Rd.
Wimberley, TX 78676

Member BBB Online 2005

Subject: An unusual plea: Help Me Stop Rita

As I type these words, people in Houston are scrambling to leave the city.

The mayor has urged many to evacuate.

The next hurricane, Rita, is bigger and badder than Katrina, and it's headed this way.

Yes, our area is in the path of the hurricane, too.

With luck, by the time it hits mainland Texas, it will have dropped from a category 5 to a category 1 hurricane. We're stocking up on supplies, like everyone else.

While the world is still reeling from the effects of Katrina, we're now bracing for something that could be just as bad, or worse.

As I listen to the news and watch people, the key word that everyone says or seems to breathe is *victim.*

We're victims of storms.

We're victims of chance.

We're victims of a poorly run government.

We're victims of gas prices, gas shortages, inflation, recession, taxes, wars, and now—the worst of all—Mother Nature.

I'm going to say something unusual. It may upset some people. I'm hoping it will inspire you. Here goes:

You have more power than you think. While you may not want to stand in the path of Rita, you don't have to cower under the bed.

As odd as it may sound, I believe that if enough of us think positive, we can create a counterstorm of sorts. We can protect ourselves and our loved ones with our thoughts.

I've described and proved this with the research in the back of my book, *The Attractor Factor*. Nineteen studies *proved* that when a large group of people hold positive intentions, those intentions radiate out and become reality.

No, I'm not saying ignore the storm warnings. I'm saying don't get caught up in the fear that the warnings often trigger.

Look. If you think the storm will get you, then it's already gotten you. You're living in fear. Your life is dark, gloomy, and in a cage. The media is flawless at whipping us into fear.

So I suggest ignoring the media. It's not information, it's propaganda. It gets large groups of people to think negative, which, of course, then becomes reality.

Why can't we do the opposite?

Why can't we get large groups of people to think positive?

At this very moment, as I type this and you read this, all is well.

Isn't it?

Aren't you okay?

Aren't you feeling fine right now?

Yes, be sure to have batteries and water and supplies.

But also check the storehouse in your mind.

Are you living in fear or living in trust?

Are you focused on the negative, or are you doing something to create a positive?

We are all, always, at choice.

My plea is that the readers of my e-zine—you—will stop, breathe, and focus; pray, or in some other positive way send out an energy that will help dissolve the fear in and around us.

I'm asking you to do this on Saturday, the day Rita is scheduled to visit Texas.

As I was finishing this article, UPS delivered two books to me. Both are timely and worth mentioning.

Unconditional Bliss by Howard Raphael Cushnir says you can find happiness in the face of hardship.

I think this is relevant. While the media are making us shake in our boots, we can choose to take care of ourselves and others *while* remaining happy.

Happiness is a choice.

The other book looks just as fascinating. It's *Megatrends 2010* by Pat Aburdene.

To my surpirse (and delight) the book declares that the future will be more focused on spirit.

Well, let's create the future right now. Let's focus on spirit.

What I'm asking you to do is be happy, right now. Smile. Send that loving energy out, in the direction of Texas. Intend for all to be well, for, in reality, all is well.

In fact, pretend you are the eye of the hurricane. That's the center where all is at peace. *Be* that peace and send that peace from the eye to the hurricane itself, imagining it dropping in intensity.

We can make a difference.

It begins with you.

What will you choose to think?

* *

Dr. Joe Vitale is the author of way too many books to list here. His latest title is *The Attractor Factor: 5 Easy Steps for Creating Wealth (or anything else) from the Inside Out.* It's in all book stores and available from Amazon, too. Register for Dr. Vitale's complimentary e-zine at http://www.mrfire.com. See his Katrina drive at http://www.OperationSuperHero.com.

* *

* *

Hypnotic Marketing Inc.
121 Canyon Gap Rd.
Wimberley, TX 78676
Member BBB Online 2005

Subject: Gift: How to reprogram your brain

Jason Mangrum just created online software based on the #1 best-selling book *The Attractor Factor*. It's inspiring, easy, fun, and best of all—yours freee.

The program is online, so there's nothing to download.

It walks you through the five steps, helps you get clear on what you want, guides you to release whatever may be in the way of achieving your desire, and then sends your request right into the universe.

The rest, as they say, is magic.

I tried the program and love it. Even though I'm the author of *The Attractor Factor* and expected this software to be fluff, I instead found it to be a type of online coach. It sums up the entire book in a few minutes. I'm impressed. I'm going to have a blast using this every day.

And get this: Skye (Jason's beautiful wife) just added audio to the online software. Her sweet voice makes the online program a living delight to experience.

Jason created this as a gift to you and me. Enjoy it, and be sure to invite friends to use it, too. It's at http://www.Use ManifestSoftware.com.

Go for it.

Dr. Joe Vitale
President, Hypnotic Marketing, Inc.
Creator, www.HypnoticMarketingStrategy.com.
Author of way too many books to mention here.
See www.MrFire.com or www.Amazon.com.

THE SECRETS

1. Create relationships first: People buy from people they like and trust.
2. Practice karmic marketing: Give now, knowing it will return later.
3. Write hypnotically: People are bombed with e-mails, so yours needs to rivet.
4. Share your personality: Be ruthlessly honest about who you are.
5. Get out of your ego: Think of what the traffic wants, not what you want to sell.

BIBLIOGRAPHY

Anonymous. *Dynamic Speed Hypnosis*. Escondido, CA: The Master Hypnotist, 1956.

Alsop, Ronald. *The Wall Street Journal on Marketing*. New York: New American Library, 1986.

Bacon, Mark. *Write Like the Pros: Using the Secrets of Ad Writers and Journalists in Business*. Hoboken, NJ: John Wiley & Sons, 1988.

Bandler, Richard, and John Grinder. *Frogs into Princes: Neuro-Linguistic Programming*. Moab, UT: Real People Press, 1979.

———. *The Structure of Magic: A Book about Language and Therapy*. Palo Alto, CA: Science and Behavior Books, 1975.

———. *Trance-formations: Neuro-Linguistic Programming and the Structure of Hypnosis*. Moab, UT: Real People Press, 1981.

Blakeslee, Thomas. *Beyond the Conscious Mind: Unlocking the Secrets of the Self*. Lincoln, NE: iUniverse, 1996.

Block, Lawrence. *Write for Your Life: The Book about the Seminar*. Ft. Myers Beach, FL: Write for Your Life, 1986.

Brown, Peter. *The Hypnotic Brain: Hypnotherapy and Social Communication*. New Haven, CT: Yale University Press, 1991.

Burton, John. *Hypnotic Language: Its Structure and Use*. Carmarthen, UK: Crown House, 2000.

———. *States of Equilibrium*. Carmarthen, UK: Crown House, 2003.

Caples, John. *How to Make Your Advertising Make Money*. Englewood Cliffs, NJ: Prentice-Hall, 1983.

———. *Tested Advertising Methods*. Englewood Cliffs, NJ: Prentice-Hall, 1974.

Carr, Allen. *The Easy Way to Stop Smoking*. New York: Sterling, 2004.

Charvet, Shelle Rose. *Words That Change Minds: Mastering the Language of Influence*. Dubuque, IA: Kendall/Hunt, 1995.

Collier, Robert. *The Robert Collier Letter Book*. Oak Harbor, WA: Robert Collier Publications, 1937.

Conklin, Robert. *The Power of a Magnetic Personality*. New York: Parker, 1965.

Considine, Ray, and Murray Raphel. *The Great Brain Robbery: A Collection of Proven Ideas to Make Money and Change Your Life*. Altadena, CA: Great Brain Robbery, 1980.

Glassner, Selma. *The Analogy Book of Related Words: Your Secret Shortcut to Power Writing*. Buena Vista, CO: Communication Creativity, 1990.

Gordon, David. *Phoenix: Therapeutic Patterns of Milton H. Erickson*. Cupertino, CA: Meta Publications, 1981.

Edmonston, William, Jr. *The Induction of Hypnosis*. New York: John Wiley & Sons, 1986.

Elman, Dave. *Hypnotherapy*. Glendale, CA: Westwood Publishing, 1964.

Erickson, Betty Alice. *Milton H. Erickson, M.D.: An American Healer*. Sedona, AZ: Ringling Rocks Press, 2006.

Estabrooks, George. *Hypnotism*. New York: Dutton, 1943.

Flesch, Rudolf. *The Art of Readable Writing*. New York: Harper & Row, 1959.

Foxall, Gordon. *Marketing Psychology: The Paradigm in the Wings*. New York: Palgrave, 1997.

Frankel, Fred. *Hypnosis: Trance as a Coping Mechanism*. New York: Plenum, 1976.

Fromm, Erika. *Contemporary Hypnosis Research*. New York: Guilford Press, 1992.

Gafner, George. *Hypnotic Techniques for Standard Psychotherapy and Formal Hypnosis.* New York: Norton, 2003.

Gallwey, Timothy. *The Inner Game of Tennis.* New York: Random House, 1997.

Garfinkel, David. *Advertising Headlines That Make You Rich.* Long Island, NY: MorganJames, 2006.

Garn, Roy. *The Magic Power of Emotional Appeal.* Englewood Cliffs, NJ: Prentice-Hall, 1960.

Gauld, Alan. *A History of Hypnotism.* New York: Cambridge University Press, 1992.

Glasser, Selma. *The Analogy Book of Related Words: Your Secret Shortcut to Power Writing.* Buena Vista, CO: Communication Creativity, 1990.

Godefroy, Christian, and Dominique Glocheux. *How to Write Letters that Sell: Winning Techniques for Achieving Sales through Direct Mail.* London: Piatkus, 1994.

Goode, Kenneth. *Advertising.* New York: Greenberg, 1932.

Gordon, David. *Therapeutic Metaphors.* Cupertino, CA: Meta, 1978.

Grambs, David. *The Describer's Dictionary.* New York: Norton, 1993.

Green, Barry, and Timothy Gallwey. *The Inner Game of Music.* New York: Doubleday, 1986.

Gross, John. *Aphorisms.* New York: Oxford University Press, 1987.

Grothe, Mardy. *Never Let a Fool Kiss You or a Kiss Fool You: Word Play for Word Lovers.* New York: Penguin, 1999.

Haley, Jay. *Jay Haley on Milton H. Erickson.* Bristol, PA: Brunner/Mazel, 1993.

Hammond, Corydon. *Handbook of Hypnotic Suggestions and Metaphors.* New York: Norton, 1990.

Hatch, Denison. *Million Dollar Mailings.* Washington, DC: Libey Publishing, 1992.

Havens, Ronald. *The Wisdom of Milton H. Erickson: The Complete Volume.* Carmarthen, UK: Crown House, 2003.

Heller, Steven. *Monsters and Magical Sticks: There's No Such Thing as Hypnosis?* Tempe, AZ: New Falcon, 1987.

Hilgard, Ernest. *Hypnotic Susceptibility.* New York: Harcourt, Brace & World, 1965.

Hogan, Kevin. *Covert Hypnosis.* Eagan, MN: Network 3000, 2001.

———. *The Psychology of Persuasion: How to Persuade Others to Your Way of Thinking.* Greta, LA: Pelican, 1996.

———. *The Science of Influence.* Hoboken, NJ: John Wiley & Sons, 2006.

Hogan, Kevin. *Through the Open Door: Secrets of Self-Hypnosis.* Greta, LA: Pelican, 2000.

Honek, Water. *My Amazing Discovery.* Austin, TX: Beta Books, 1993.

Izard, Carroll. *The Psychology of Emotions.* New York: Plenum, 1991.

Joyner, Mark. *The Irresistible Offer: How to Sell Your Product or Service in 3 Seconds or Less.* Hoboken, NJ: John Wiley & Sons, 2005.

Kennedy, Dan. *The Ultimate Sales Letter.* Holbrook, MA: Adams Media, 1990.

Kocina, Lonny. *Media Hypnosis: Unleashing the Most Powerful Sales Tool on Earth.* Minneapolis, MN: Mid-America Entertainment, 2002.

Ledochowski, Igor. *The Deep Trance Training Manual, Vol. 1.* Carmarthen UK: Crown House, 2003.

Lentz, John. *How the Word Heals: Hypnosis in Scriptures.* Lincoln, NE: iUniverse, 2002.

Levy, Mark. *The Accidental Genius: Revolutionize Your Thinking through Private Writing.* San Francisco: Berrett-Koehler, 2000.

McGill, Ormond. *The New Encyclopedia of Stage Hypnotism.* Carmarthen, UK: Crown House, 1996.

McKee, Robert. *Story: Substance, Structure, Style, and the Principles of Screenwriting.* New York: Reagan Books, 1997.

McLauchlin, Larry. *Advanced Language Patterns Mastery.* Calgary, Canada: Leading Edge Communications, 1992.

Miller, Anne. *Metaphorically Selling: How to Use the Magic of Metaphors to Sell, Persuade and Explain Anything to Anyone.* New York: Chiron Associates, 2004.

Moine, Donald, and Kenneth Lloyd. *Unlimited Selling Power: How to Master Hypnotic Selling Skills.* Upper Saddle River, NJ: Prentice-Hall, 1990.

Murphy, Gardner. *An Outline of Abnormal Psychology*. New York: Modern Library, 1929.

Nicholas, Ted. *How to Turn Words into Money*. Indian Rocks Beach, FL: Nicholas Direct, Inc., 2003.

O'Hanlon, William Hudson. *Solution-Oriented Hypnosis: An Ericksonian Approach*. New York: Norton, 1992.

Petrie, Sidney, and Robert Stone. *How to Strengthen Your Life with Mental Isometrics*. New York: Parker, 1967.

Plous, Scott. *The Psychology of Judgment and Decision Making*. New York: McGraw-Hill, 1993.

Rosen, Sidney. *My Voice Will Go with You: The Teaching Tales of Milton H. Erickson*. New York: Norton, 1982.

Sarno, John. *The Divided Mind: The Epidemic of Mindbody Disorders*. New York: Reagan Books, 2006.

———. *Healing Back Pain: The Mind-Body Connection*. New York: Warner Books, 1991.

Schank, Roger. *Tell Me a Story: Narrative and Intelligence*. Evanston, IL: Northwestern University Press, 2005.

Schwab, Victor. *How to Write a Good Advertisement: A Short Course in Copywriting*. Hollywood, CA: Wilshire Books, 1962.

Schwartz, Eugene. *Breakthrough Advertising*. Stamford, CT: Bottom Line Books, 2004.

Silvester, Trevor. *WordWeaving: The Science of Suggestion*. Cambs, UK: Quest, 2003.

Simmons, Annette. *The Story Factor: Inspiration, Influence, and Persuasion through the Art of Storytelling*. Cambridge, MA: Perseus, 2001.

Snyder, Edward. *Hypnotic Poetry: A Study of Trance-Inducing Technique in Certain Poems and Its Literary Significance*. Philadelphia, PA: University of Pennsylvania Press, 1924.

Sommer, Elyse. *As One Mad with Wine and Other Similes*. New York: Visible Ink, 1991.

Stevenson, Michael. *Learn Hypnosis . . . Now! The Easiest Way to Learn Hypnosis*. Laguna Hills, CA: Liquid Mirror Enterprises, 2005.

St. James, Martin. *Sleep You Bastard! The True Misadventures of the World's Greatest Hypnotist.* Melbourne, Australia: Spellbound Promotions, 1993.

St. John, Noah. *Permission to Succeed: Unlocking the Mystery of Success Anorexia.* Deerfield Beach, FL: Health Communications, Inc., 1999.

Straus, Roger. *Creative Self-Hypnosis.* Lincoln, NE: iUniverse, 2000.

Streeter, Michael. *Hypnosis: Secrets of the Mind.* New York: Barron's, 2004.

Sugarman, Joseph. *Advertising Secrets of the Written Word.* Las Vegas, NV: DelStar, 1998.

Sugarman, Joseph. *Triggers: 30 Sales Tools You Can Use to Control the Mind of Your Prospect to Motivate, Influence and Persuade.* Las Vegas, NV: DelStar, 1999.

Sweet, Robert Burdette. *Writing Towards Wisdom: The Writer as Shaman.* Carmichael, CA: Helios House, 1990.

Thompson, Peter. *Persuading Aristotle: The Timeless Art of Persuasion in Business, Negotiation and the Media.* Melbourne, Australia: Allen and Unwin, 1998.

Vitale, Joe. *The AMA Complete Guide to Small Business Advertising.* Lincolnwood, IL: NTC Business Books, 1995.

———. *The Attractor Factor: Five Easy Steps for Creating Wealth (or Anything Else) from the Inside Out.* Hoboken, NJ: John Wiley & Sons, 2005.

———. *Life's Missing Instruction Manual: The Guidebook You Should Have Been Given at Birth.* Hoboken, NJ: John Wiley & Sons, 2006.

———. *The Seven Lost Secrets of Success.* Long Island, NY: MorganJames, 2005.

———. *There's a Customer Born Every Minute: P.T. Barnum's 10 Rings of Power for Fame, Fortune and Building an Empire.* Hoboken, NJ: John Wiley & Sons, 2006.

———. *Turbocharge Your Writing.* Houston, TX: Awareness Publications, 1992.

———. *Zen and the Art of Writing.* Westcliff, CA: Westcliff, 1984.

Wallas, Lee. *Stories for the Third Ear: Using Hypnotic Fables in Psychotherapy*. New York: Norton, 1985.

Walsh, Brian. *Unleashing Your Brilliance*. Victoria, Canada: Walsh Seminars, 2005.

Warren, Blair. *The Forbidden Keys to Persuasion*. San Antonio, TX: Warren Productions, 2003.

Waterfield, Robin. *Hidden Depths: The Story of Hypnosis*. New York: Macmillan, 2002.

Wells, Wesley. *An Outline of Abnormal Psychology*. N.p.: 1929.

Williams, Roy. *Secret Formulas of the Wizard of Ads*. Austin, TX: Bard Press, 1999.

Wind, Yoram, and Colin Crook. *The Power of Impossible Thinking*. Upper Saddle River, NJ: Wharton School Publishing, 2005.

Wolinsky, Stephen. *Trances People Live: Healing Approaches in Quantum Psychology*. Falls Village, CT: Bramble, 1991.

Zarren, Jordan. *Brief Cognitive Hypnosis*. New York: Springer, 2002.

Zeig, Jeffrey. *Experiencing Erickson: An Introduction to the Man and His Work*. Bristol, PA: Brunner/Mazel, 1985.

———. *The Letters of Milton H. Erickson*. Phoenix, AZ: Zeig, Tucker & Theisen Publishers, 2000.

INDEX

253

About Dr. Joe Vitale

Dr. Joe Vitale is President of Hypnotic Marketing, Inc., and author of way too many books to list here, including the #1 best-selling books *The Attractor Factor* and *Life's Missing Instruction Manual,* and the best-selling Nightingale-Conant audioprogram, *The Power of Outrageous Marketing.*

His latest books include: *There's a Customer Born Every Minute, Meet and Grow Rich, The Greatest Money-Making Secret in History, Adventures Within,* and *The E-Code.* His next book will be *Buying Trances.*

He also created a software program to help you write sales letters, ads, news releases, speeches, and even entire books using his Hypnotic Writing methods. You can learn more about it at http://www.HypnoticWritingWizard.com.

You can sign up to receive Dr. Vitale's free monthly e-newsletter, "News You Can Use!" at his main web site at http://www.mrfire.com.

HOW CAN YOU EASILY BECOME A MORE POWERFUL HYPNOTIC WRITER?

Get Joe Vitale's
Hypnotic Writing Wizard software

For more details see
www.HypnoticWritingWizard.com